The
Fragile
Presence

The Fragile Presence

TRANSCENDENCE
IN MODERN
LITERATURE

by JOHN KILLINGER

FORTRESS PRESS   Philadelphia

Grateful acknowledgment is made to the following for permission to quote from the indicated works:

To The Bobbs-Merrill Company, Inc., Indianapolis, Indiana, for quotations from *Black Magic Poetry 1961-1967*, Copyright © 1969, by LeRoi Jones.

To The Dial Press, New York, New York, for quotations from *Another Country*, Copyright © 1960, 1962 by James Baldwin; from *Blues for Mr. Charlie*, Copyright © 1964 by James Baldwin; from *Go Tell It On the Mountain*, Copyright © 1952, 1953 by James Baldwin; and from *Tell Me How Long the Train's Been Gone*, Copyright © 1968 by James Baldwin.

To Doubleday & Co., Inc., New York, New York, for quotations from "The Abyss," Copyright © 1963 by Beatrice Roethke as administratrix of the estate of Theodore Roethke; "Words for the Wind," Copyright © 1955 by Theodore Roethke both from *The Collected Poems of Theodore Roethke*.

To Faber & Faber, Ltd., London, England, for a quotation from N. F. Simpson, *A Resounding Tinkle*, 1958.

To Grove Press, Inc., New York, New York, for quotations from Alain Robbe-Grillet, *For a New Novel*, Copyright © 1965 by Grove Press, Inc.; from Richard Brautigan, *A Confederate General from Big Sur*, Copyright © 1964 by Richard Brautigan; from Henry Miller, *Tropic of Cancer*, Copyright © 1961 by Grove Press, Inc.; from Samuel Beckett, *Krapp's Last Tape and Other Dramatic Pieces*, Copyright © 1957 by Samuel Beckett, Copyright © 1958, 1959, 1960 by Grove Press, Inc.; and from Hugh Kenner, *Samuel Beckett*, Copyright © 1961 by Hugh Kenner.

To Harper & Row, Publishers, Inc., New York, New York, for quotations from Richard Wright, *Native Son* (Perennial Edition, pp. 329-30 and 390), Copyright © 1940 by Richard Wright; renewed 1968 by Ellen Wright.

To the Ronald Hobbs Literary Agency, New York, New York, and the authors for quotations from the works of Yusef Iman, Bobb Hamilton, Ben Caldwell, and Charles Anderson in *Black Fire*, edited by LeRoi Jones and Larry Neal (New York: William Morrow and Co., 1969), Copyright © 1968 by Yusef Iman, Bobb Hamilton, Ben Caldwell, and Charles Anderson.

To Alfred A. Knopf, Inc., New York, New York, for a quotation from "Sunday Morning" in *The Collected Poems of Wallace Stevens*, Copyright © 1923, 1951 by Wallace Stevens.

To The J. B. Lippincott Company, Philadelphia, Pennsylvania, for a quotation from *A Rap on Race* by Margaret Mead and James Baldwin, Copyright © 1971 by Margaret Mead and James Baldwin.

To New Directions Publishing Corp., New York, New York, for quotations from Henry Miller, *The Wisdom of the Heart*, Copyright © 1941 by New Directions Publishing Corporation.

To Stein and Day Publishers, New York, New York, for a quotation from *Waiting for the End*, Copyright © 1964 by Leslie A. Fiedler.

To The University of Notre Dame Press, Notre Dame, Indiana, for a quotation from Frederick J. Hoffman, *The Imagination's New Beginning*, 1967.

To The Viking Press, Inc., New York, New York, for quotations from *The Rainbow* by D. H. Lawrence, Copyright © 1915 by D. H. Lawrence, 1943 by Frieda Lawrence; and from "The Fox" from *The Portable D. H. Lawrence*, ed. by Diana Trilling, Copyright © 1923 by Thomas B. Seltzer Inc., 1951 by Frieda Lawrence.

To
NATHAN A. SCOTT, JR.
with affection
and gratitude
for a dozen years
of friendship
and
a lifetime
of
enrichment

Contents

Introduction   1

I. Reverberations of Job:
    God in the Literature of Anguish   11

II. Camus and After: God in the Literature
    of Absurdity   49

III. Fulfillment as Carnal: God in the
    Literature of Sensuality   79

IV. Reaping the Whirlwind: God in the
    Literature of the Black Experience   125

Epilogue   159

Index   163

Acknowledgments

Some of the ideas and materials in this book were originally presented in lectures given in the Union Church of Guatemala before the ministers of English-speaking churches in the Caribbean area. Pastor and Mrs. Lloyd Jacobson were my special hosts for the occasion, and I have bright memories of their vivacity and kindness, as well as of the colorful Indian marketplaces and mirrorlike lakes of that remarkably beautiful country. My old friend Garth Thompson of San Juan, Puerto Rico, doubtless had something to do with my being invited to visit with this stimulating group of churchmen, and I owe him yet another debt of thanks.

I was further motivated to develop the manuscript of the book when the invitation came to deliver the Annual Lectures for 1970 at Lexington Theological Seminary. The weather was not so cooperative as in Guatemala—a six-inch crust of ice covered the rolling Bluegrass—but the warm hospitality of President and Mrs. W. A. Welsh and their splendid faculty more than atoned for that. The second essay, "Camus and After," later appeared in the *Lexington Theological Quarterly* for October 1970, ably edited by Professor William R. Barr.

The final essay, "Reaping the Whirlwind," has gotten even more mileage. After being given as a lecture at Lexington Theological Seminary, it was again delivered in convocations at the University of Louisville and at Samford University in Birmingham, where, as on previous occasions, I enjoyed the impeccable kindness of President Leslie Wright and his associates. Subsequently published under the title of "The Black

Man and the White God" in the Winter 1970 issue of *Religion and Life*, which is edited by my good friend Jean Hager, it was also chosen by the Office of the Chief of Chaplains in Washington, D.C., for reprinting and distribution to military chaplains.

The completed manuscript was at last submitted to a hearing before my seminar in Theology and Literature at the Divinity School of Vanderbilt University. My students, as I am quick to say to them, are more than students—they are colleagues. Their advice, reactions, and insights are priceless to me in the shaping of thought and honing of expression. I often pinch myself in amazement that I should be paid a salary for sitting down to talk with them about such matters as are enclosed in these covers. But that is my glad situation, and I am grateful for it.

The Divinity School
Vanderbilt University
August 14, 1972

Introduction

A few years ago it was customary for the writer undertaking a theological assessment of modern letters to deplore the phenomenon of the *deus absconditus* or absentee God among recent authors. It was easy enough, as I myself found in writing *The Failure of Theology in Modern Literature*, to cite Nietzsche and Hardy and Schreiner and Eliot and Hemingway and Faulkner and Sartre and Camus and to conclude that there was a monstrous titanism in the air which was not only antichurch but anti-God. More than a few times, in my barnstorming expeditions around the university lecturing circuit, I used a particularly quotable tidbit from Edmund Fuller's *Man in Modern Fiction*: "Our present generations now practicing the art of fiction are the first generations in which there have been large, influential, and admired groups of novelists working, in many instances quite unconsciously, on the tacit or declared premise that there is no God, basing the patterns of their work on the implications, again often unconscious, that arise out of that premise."[1] This word seemed to sum it up perfectly. Modern man was in self-exile from a sense of the holy and the numinous.

In the meantime much theology has gone under the bridge —and perhaps much pseudotheology too. Tillich's idea of correlation, that religion and culture are intimately bound to one another and must be understood in terms of one another, finally permeated a whole generation of younger theologians. Bonhoeffer's *Letters and Papers from Prison*, with the peculiar force of any timely word inscribed in a martyr's blood,

1. Edmund Fuller, *Man in Modern Fiction* (New York: Random House, 1958), p. 8.

contributed to a massive resecularization program. Harvey Cox's *The Secular City* helped to bring the program to floodtide. Bishop Robinson's little book *Honest to God*, heavily reliant on the ideas of Tillich, Bonhoeffer, and Bultmann, found an excited and sympathetic reception from many thousands of persons, Christian and non-Christian alike, who tended to be drawn together by his words assuring them that "men who are Christians find themselves on the same side as those who are not. And among one's intelligent non-Christian friends one discovers many who are far nearer to the Kingdom of heaven than they themselves can credit. For while they imagine they have rejected the Gospel, they have in fact largely been put off by a particular way of thinking about the world which quite legitimately they find incredible."[2] Then came that dramatic little revolution which needed both the naïveté and the *éclat* of American entrepreneurs to have come off at all, the Death of God movement, whose unacknowledged effect on theological work in this country has been all out of proportion to the academic prestige of its advocates. And, all the while, a *theologia incognito* was taking shape in the discourse of Marshall McLuhan, Tom Wolfe, Eric Hoffer, Edward T. Hall, Norman O. Brown, Abraham Maslow, Timothy Leary, and Herbert Marcuse, as well as from the works of such redivivus figures as Aldous Huxley and Hermann Hesse.

Now it is possible to see clearly what I feel I was awfully slow to see, that an almost total theological inversion has been occurring. The God many of us talked about so comfortably and knowingly a decade or two ago was even then an anachronism, a carryover from too many philosophies and theologies which bloomed and faded in distant eras. We have had to reconceive him—often with inward pain and awkwardness—along more radically current lines. We see now that his reality, to us, is directly related to our ability to perceive him in the outrageously new and secular aspects of our existence. We are learning to have more confidence in current visions and to depend less heavily upon the bartered achievements of tradition. We suspect that it is a time for radical surgery, when we shall be saved only by severing ourselves from those bloated and schleroid organs or appendices which, contrary to the belief of some that they are vital to our well-being, are actually poisoning our systems with a deadly and bilious venom. Our only danger is not that we shall be too radical but that we shall not be radical enough.

What we see also is that literature has once more beat us to the draw.

It has a way of doing that in every age. Martin Jarrett-Kerr reminded us of this with a piquant image drawn from Virgil Gheorghiu's novel *La vingt-cinquième heure*. Gheorghiu's hero, himself a novelist, describes how underwater sailors once took white rabbits aboard their vessels to warn them of any dangerous reduction of oxygen. At the moment when the atmosphere became poisonous the rabbits died, and the men knew they had no more than five or six hours to live. The artist, said Father Jarrett-Kerr, is the white rabbit of society; he feels before others the atmospheric changes which will affect us all a little later.[3]

We knew that this was true of writers in the nineteenth century. Melville, Dostoevsky, Baudelaire, even Mark Twain, fought then most of the theological battles which we have had to face in the last fifty years. Most readers and critics did not at the time realize this with any seriousness. To them these preternaturally dark creators (excepting Twain, of course, whom they misknew completely) were convulsed by madness, or seemed to be struggling with some invisible, nihilistic monster which had them entwined in its tentacles. Now we are able to make out the shape of the monster, and to see that its nature was both cosmic and spiritual, that the

3. Martin Jarrett-Kerr, *The Secular Promise* (Philadelphia: Fortress Press, 1964), pp. 148–49.

lightning of numinosity which we still behold electrifying their night-and-wind-tossed skies was really the crackling of divine presence as they invaded and desecrated ancient sanctuaries. We read them with respect and humility, and perhaps with just a touch of envy that the lines of battle should have been drawn for them so taut and clear.

We did *not* see that the increasingly secularized and theologically indifferent or "confused" writers of the twentieth century actually presaged a healthy new individualism in theology—an individualism of the kind Sam Keen describes when he says, "If I am to rediscover the holy, it must be in *my* biography and not in the history of Israel."[4] Now, with this individualism upon us, we are casting fresh glances at the very poets and playwrights and novelists whom we had considered most antithetical to religion, and are finding them neither so untheological nor so reprobate as we once assumed. Even the moribund characters of Beckett, to name an extreme example, impart their priestly truth. I have made my own apology for the obtuseness of my earlier book,[5] and others have made theirs. Now we are all busy recovering the ground we so insensitively hurried across before, relistening to the voices we could not hear then because we had not learned to trust the sound of our own voices, and discovering epiphanies we had no idea existed because we were blinded by our gross idolatries.

Frederick Hoffman, the author of a superlative study of Beckett, has said in a recent book that all the evidence from modern writings bespeaks a continued thrust toward universals despite the absolute necessity of expressing private visions. "Twentieth-century literature has been produced in a time of redefinitions, in which the burden of proof concerning reality appears to rest with the individual artist."[6] Changes in

4. Sam Keen, *To a Dancing God* (New York: Harper and Row, 1970), p. 99.
5. Cf. "Mythos und Ritual als Urgrund der Literatur und Theologie," *Internationale Dialog Zeitschrift* 4 (January 1969): 319–30.
6. Frederick J. Hoffman, *The Imagination's New Beginning* (Notre Dame: University of Notre Dame Press, 1967), p. 9.

style, experimental forms of writing, are themselves evidences
of the struggle, of the poet's search "in a whirl of particulars
for standards of universal form, for the stillness about which
the world moves." Two general characteristics seem to arise
from this condition: an extraordinary mixture of doubt and
assertion, and a tendency to exalt the "thing" above the
universal.

Two principal metaphors [in turn] seem to engage all serious
writers who concern themselves with both of these matters: the
first, the Incarnation, is a major desideratum (that is, for the
most part the "man of imagination" seeks a transcending means
and a universal source); the second involves the validity of
things, sensed as the result of an effort to present their precise
"dinglichkeit" as vividly as possible. How these two come together makes for interesting speculation. There is what Hillis
Miller calls the "new immediacy," in which the comprehensible
particular survives the loss of a transcending power. The tendency is strong in our time to separate metaphor from doctrine,
or to give metaphor an arcanic power. It does not argue a lack
of faith so much as a loss of tried and true ways of manifesting
it. Theological necessities are as strong as ever; the desire for
transcendence remains. Literature is as important a resource
for the metaphoric elaboration of the theological view as it ever
was, and the variety of ways in which metaphysical questions
are first framed and then answered is a part of the brilliant
kaleidoscope that is modern literature.[7]

The primary difference between our time and all previous
situations is that the search is now a more personal one. The
imagination rules with unusual activity, and there is little
inclination to settle for "preordained" metaphors. But the
quotient of religious imagination is "stronger perhaps than it
has been in most literatures, because of the need to establish
new formulations of the central theological metaphors."[8]

The quest for a new transcendence *in* and *through* the
materialities of human existence is unspeakably important.

7. Ibid., p. 10.
8. Ibid., p. 16.

There is no way of estimating what it has done and is doing to revitalize the metaphor of incarnation even in theological circles. We are plunging deeper toward the point of the vortex where flesh and spirit are fused, and carrying more with us in the path, than ever before in public history. The theophanies may be minuter and subtler than before, and even more anonymous—Mallarmé once said, "To name an object is to do away with three-quarters of the enjoyment. To suggest it, to evoke it—that is what charms the imagination"— but they are also more numerous. Liturgical dramas of the sort Eliot gave us in *Murder in the Cathedral* are too structured, too dependent on medieval order, for many playgoers today, whose sensibilities are closer to the disparate, subliturgical qualities of *Waiting for Godot.* Yet there is a touch of mystery, of unsettledness, about the latter which may offer more possibility for true incarnation than Eliot gave us in his marvelous play. It has to do with what Nathan A. Scott, Jr., talked about in his book of the Keatsian title, *Negative Capability*—with a strong disinclination to try to subdue or resolve "what is recalcitrantly indeterminate and ambiguous in the human scene of our time" or to "reach irritably after any great counterpoise to chaos."[9] There is a patience before the *intransigeance* of corporeal existence that has rarely if ever before been exhibited in the spiritual awareness of man. Joyce, Kafka, Beckett, Grass, Brautigan do not push for early resolutions of the metaphorical problem, but are willing to wait, interminably if need be, for what *appears.* If we are bothered by their irresolution, it may be that we are guilty of having reached irritably after the counterpoise to chaos and have settled for a cheaply spiritualized sense of what incarnation is really about.

Professor Heidegger, in his recently translated essays on language, underlines the importance of *waiting* to knowing and of not rushing ahead in the vain expectancy of precipi-

9. Nathan A. Scott, Jr., *Negative Capability: Studies in the New Literature and the Religious Situation* (New Haven: Yale University Press, 1970), p. xiv.

tating answers to the great human enigmas. He appears to have been particularly affected by oriental thought, which has long had a kind of creative patience instilled at its core. We need more reverence, he says, for what the Chinese poet Laotse meant by *Tao* or "the way." We are prone to think of a way as a mere stretch with two fixed ends, and to want to rush from where we are to the other end. If we do that, however, we have not really left where we were; we have merely brought the other end to us. Being "in the way" involves a certain indeterminacy, a suspendedness, in which we are capable of being taught. The paradox is caught momentarily in a bit of dialogue between Professor Heidegger (designated "I") and a Japanese guest, Professor Tezuka of the Imperial University of Tokyo (designated "J"):

> I: But it seems to me that, in the field in which we are moving, we reach those things with which we are originally familiar precisely if we do not shun passing through things strange to us.
>
> J: In what sense do you understand "originally familiar"? You do not mean what we know first, do you?
>
> I: No—but what before all else has been entrusted to our nature, and becomes known only at the last.[10]

That is, we cannot even know penetratingly what we have already known, or what has been given to us by our culture, until we have passed through the world as if they had not been given to us at all.

This, it seems to me, is what the poets of our time are courageously attempting to practice. In the modern world which Eliot described in *The Waste Land*, where no one knows for sure "the roots that clutch" or the branches that grow "out of this stony rubbish" of civilization, they have come in under the shadow of the red rock and are looking at

10. Martin Heidegger, *On the Way to Language*, trans. P. D. Hertz (New York: Harper and Row, 1971), p. 33.

"fear in a handful of dust." And looking, bless them, *without flinching.* As Robert Martin Adams has illustrated so adroitly in his book entitled *Nil,* they have stared unremittingly into nothingness, the void, *le néant,* until they have forced it to become the veritable substance of a new experience.[11] "Our nada which art in nada" pushes "Our Father which art in heaven" into a dimension beyond the one we have known. The world that was known and charted opens onto another whose prospects are terrifying in their strangeness.

The theologian in the face of all this cannot simply renounce his vocation as theologian. Regardless of his temptation to do so, he cannot turn over to the artist the responsibility he has to comment upon the artist's vision, helping even the artist to understand what he has done. He remains a kind of historian of religious culture, as it were, to observe the relationships between the visions of one age and the visions of another. I am reminded of this quite forcefully by a letter which came into my hands during the writing of the preceding paragraphs. The sender of the letter, a former colleague, writes:

> As much as I agree with you in what you write and speak, we differ on the matter of religious faith. You have it, and I don't. I am not necessarily an atheist; rather, you might label me a free-thinker. Influential on me in this regard have been Matthew Arnold, J. S. Mill, Thomas Hardy, T. H. Huxley, Keats, Shelley, Fitzgerald, Housman, Tennyson, Shakespeare, Gray, and others. My conclusions are that the Bible is a great work of literature but in no sense the infallible word of God. Jesus of Nazareth is one of history's most attractive characters, but not the son of God, for very probably there is no God.
>
> In fact, I have what is called the tragic vision of man's place in the universe. As Arnold says, "We are here as on a darkling plain. . . ," destined to death when we just come to know the pleasures of life. Life, I need not tell you, is filled with injustices. Were you or I in charge of existence, we would make things much more equitable. One of the most penetrating of the quatrains of the *Rubaiyat* is this one addressed to God: "O

11. Robert Martin Adams, *Nil: Episodes in the Literary Conquest of Void During the 19th Century* (London: Oxford University Press, 1966).

thou, whom man of baser earth didst make,/ And even with Paradise, devised the snake,/ For all the sin wherewith the face of man is blackened,/ Man's forgiveness give—and take!" The last two words should be underlined. What about the homosexual, black murderer, the dope-crazed thief, the despondent, and thousands of others? They are, at least in part, the victims of circumstance yet they are judged by conventional standards bent on condemnation. I assert that if indeed there is a God, he is one who takes into account, as Burns has stated, all the factors in the situation, one who is the very antithesis to evangelical morality. If he isn't this, he isn't worth having.

There is obvious anguish in these words, an anguish partially shaped and pointed up by numerous authors aggrieved at a sense of man's finitude in a universe which appears, if not actively hostile, at least indifferent to his plight. How do I answer the letter? I could easily sympathize, without feigning, and say, "I know, for I have felt this too." But somehow I feel that my task is greater than this. Theology, to the extent that I understand what it is about, carries me beyond or above (no pride of stance is meant by the metaphor) particularized conceptions of the holy or transcendent and permits me to see that, while the holy invests or cohabits with these concrete instances of its presence, it also eludes them, refusing to be incarcerated in them. What I must offer my friend, therefore, is an interpretation of the views of the authors he has cited which will be at once fair to them and cognizant of the factors which shaped or conditioned their thinking; and the interpretation must perforce include a reference to the possibility that the God they denied was indeed no God but an idol, the calcification of a historically conditioned mode of identifying the deity which had with the passing of the original conditions become not only false but perverse and even demonic. The affirmative side of such a declaration is obvious: by freeing the transcendent from an obligation to former epiphanies, it reopens the possibilities for theophany in the present age.

What I have attempted to do in the following essays is to

bring the hermeneutical task to literature, and, without exerting pressure on the material to skew it one way or another, to ask what the possibilities are. I have tried to listen to the voices, and then, forgetting most of the details of what was said, to hear what they were really saying, what the intonations and silences and rhythms of speech imply beyond the intended meanings. On the surface there is often confusion, hurt, despair, sadness, betrayal, nihilism—quieter and honed to a finer edge, perhaps, than in the earlier figures my friend has steeped himself in, though possibly even more desperate for that reason. The soundings, however, indicate something else. They seem to be pregnant with the promise of something beyond this present sense of impasse, as though a new and richer apprehension of reality lay just the other side of a thin wall and the wall were beginning to succumb to the constant pressure upon it. I say "seem to be." The indications are not conclusive. One's reading of them is surely influenced by the hope or pessimism in one's own heart. But I, for one, am vastly encouraged. I do not see us expiring on Arnold's "darkling plain." What I see instead, with David Cassie, is "the past thrown to the freshning wind," and

> Jesus Christ
> Born in Bethlehem
> For lively lovers today.[12]

There is a footnote. Whatever saves humanity and its literature will save theology too—and vice versa—though one will not necessarily be saved through the other. The sorting of experience is primary to each. In the end, if we are lucky, it may be given us to learn the beautiful lesson which Simone Weil tried to teach us, that the way to truth often lies for each of us along lonely and difficult pathways which surprise us, in the final clearing, by converging with similar pathways taken by others. There is one God, but there are many journeys.

12. David G. Cassie, "Now Is Christmas," a Christmas verse printed by the author, 1971.

I.

Reverberations of Job:

God in the Literature of Anguish

Critics keep worrying at the connection between tragedy and religion because, as Aldous Huxley put it in *Brave New World*, there seems to be a direct relationship between suffering and God that is nowhere more discernible than in tragic literature.

Huxley's Savage, it will be recalled, was arguing with Mustapha Mond, the world controller, about the quality of life in the antiseptic new society. His own frame of reference was set primarily by Shakespeare and the Bible—especially *Lear* and *Othello*—readings no longer allowed to the public. He missed the feelings of nobility and heroism in the new man. "We prefer to do things comfortably," said the controller. "But I don't want comfort," replied Savage. "I want God, I want poetry, I want real danger, I want freedom, I want goodness. I want sin." What he really wanted, the controller pointed out, was the right to be unhappy, to grow old and ugly, to have syphilis and cancer, to be riddled with pain, and to live in constant apprehension of tomorrow. "You're welcome," said the controller.[1]

There is something crucial about Huxley's insight here, despite the snobbishness of scholars who quickly withdraw from such simple and sketchy portraits of the problem. God, or whatever the word connotes to us, does seem to belong more properly to the eras of Job and Aeschylus and Marlowe, the ages of great poetry and real danger and sin, than to our

1. Aldous Huxley, *Brave New World and Brave New World Revisited* (New York: Harper & Brothers, 1960), p. 288.

11

own technological and metaphysically tepid epoch. Mystery
having to do with the unknown, and danger and the unknown having much to do in turn with space, something has
gone out of the old humanity and the old religion with the
advent of the global village and the implosion of knowledge.
The choices posed by Huxley—suffering and God and the old
way of life vs. convenience and agnosticism and the new way
of life—may not be the only alternatives, as we shall presently
suggest, but they are certainly the logical ones, and must
therefore be explored.

Job is the touchstone, the inevitable starting point. As
Professor Sewall says in *The Vision of Tragedy*:

> It is not right to say that without the vision of life embodied
> in the Old Testament, and notably in *The Book of Job*, the
> term "tragedy" would have no substance, for the Greeks in-
> vented the term and gave it a great deal of substance. But
> knowing what we do now about the full depth and reach of
> tragedy, we can see with striking clarity in the writings of the
> ancient Hebrews the vision which we now call tragic and in
> *The Book of Job* the basic elements of the tragic form. The
> cultural situation, the matrix out of which *Job* came, is the
> very definition of "the tragic moment" in history, a period
> when traditional values begin to lose their power to comfort
> and sustain, and man finds himself once more groping in the
> dark. The unknown Poet's "action," his redoing of the ortho-
> dox and optimistic folktale of the pious and rewarded Job, is
> (as we can say now) a classic example of the dynamics of trag-
> edy, of vision creating form. And the great figure of his crea-
> tion, the suffering, questioning, and unanswered Job, is the
> towering tragic figure of antiquity. More than Prometheus or
> Oedipus, Job is the universal symbol for the western imagina-
> tion of the mystery of undeserved suffering.[2]

"Why did I not die at birth," cried Job, "come forth from
the womb and expire?" (Job 3:11). The greatest literature in

2. Richard B. Sewall, *The Vision of Tragedy* (New Haven: Yale University
Press, 1959), p. 9.

the world, by unanimous consensus, has been born of this kind of ontological misery. Wherever writing is touched by it, it becomes mysteriously deepened and hallowed. There is something about the picture of man *in extremis*, man in the depths, that is automatically truer and more revealing than the image of man in any other situation. This is why the image of the crucified One so haunts our imagination, and recurs again and again in adumbrated or symbolical form throughout human history; redemption, salvation, wholeness for man lies somehow in and through his suffering, his anguish, his realization of finitude.

And the inexplicability of the suffering, the fact that it is, as Sewall says, undeserved, lies at the heart of the attraction. *Why?* is the question that haunts man beyond all others, the plaintive emission that escapes the lips of every soul in agony. Not that the victims in tragic literature are flawless. We should have little interest in them if they were—would not even have maintained interest in the Christ through the ages after the early church's heretical teaching of his sinlessness had it not been for the confluent notion of his bearing all men's sin on the cross. They must have their faults in order for us to identify with them and enter empathetically into their anguish. As Dame Helen Gardner has observed, tragedy is as much concerned with the crimes of men as with their sufferings.[3] But the sufferings are not the direct results of specific crimes. Specific crimes may precipitate suffering, but the matter goes much deeper. It has to do with what Shakespeare in *Hamlet* referred to as an out-of-jointness belonging to the times themselves: the world, the universe, the whole of human life, existence itself gets out of phase, and harmony must be restored. Particular acts of violence, themselves the product of the overall disharmony, become the crystallizing moments in which all life, all being, is wrested back to wholeness and redemption. The great tragic figures of history are

3. Helen Gardner, *Religion and Literature* (New York: Oxford University Press, 1971), p. 22.

those whom time and destiny have elected—what St. Paul designated as *kairos* or fullness of time as opposed to mere chronological time—to suffer and set things right again.

In other words, the now rather widely held theory that tragedies may not be written in merely any age, whenever men choose to write them, but only at particular times and junctures in the history of the world when events are ripe for them, is a judicious one.[4] For, whether they are staged within a liturgical setting or not, as the Greek dramas undoubtedly were, they invariably serve a ritualistic purpose for mankind, concentrating as they do into language and designed action the *musterion* or secret which the sensibilities of man must trace in order to be cleansed and renewed for another go at life. The secret can be repeated through the ages, even clumsily, with some effect—we are still seized by the power of Aeschylus or Sophocles—but the roiling waters of time cast us up to new moments propitious for imprinting upon the public or collective mind a presently more accurate and up-to-date version.

Failure to understand this dynamic character of tragic invention probably did much to inhibit the production of tragic drama (Dame Helen reminds us that it is not necessary to say *great* tragic drama, for that is a redundancy) after the Christianization of the West, for the most vital forms of drama apparently do not flourish in periods of strong dogmatism. Shakespeare succeeded where other dramatists failed—and lives on in the manner of Job and Sophocles—because of the uniquely indomitable secularity of his mind. Although he was apparently a conforming church-attender who knew the Bible intimately in the Genevan version, which was the version used in the home and not in the church, he betrays none of the parochialisms of the orthodox mind, but ranges freely in psychic and spiritual realms, suiting his rituals to intimations transcending local and more petty theologies. The

4. Cf., e.g., Sewall, *Vision of Tragedy*, pp. 1–8, and Gardner, *Religion and Literature*, pp. 99–118.

pat but insufficient answers of most Christians to the problem of undeserved suffering did not deter him from redesigning for his and subsequent ages magnificent poetic liturgies for the celebration of that ageless human mystery. More on this matter later, and how it is related to our own resecularized and resecularizing era.

What is the secret of tragic literature and how it works? Are there ingredients which perdure, identifying real tragedy in any set of conditions which permit it to exist? Aristotle is ineluctable at this point. We always come back to him for what, paraphrasing Pope, was often rethought but ne'er so well expressed.

> Tragedy, then, is a process of imitating an action which has serious implications, is complete, and possesses magnitude; by means of language which has been made sensuously attractive, with each of its varieties found separately in the parts; enacted by the persons themselves and not presented through narrative; through a course of pity and fear completing the purification of tragic acts which have those emotional characteristics.[5]

"Imitating"—catching the rhythm of, making a ritual of. "An action which has serious implications . . . and . . . magnitude"—big enough to catch the universal. "Sensuously attractive"—made by a poet. "Enacted . . . and not presented through narrative"—entering the human sensorium, as Walter Ong would say, through sight and sound, which is more ultimate as communication than mere print or sound alone.[6] "Pity"—sympathy, involvement in the condition, the situation, the *pathos* and the *agon* of the character born to set the times aright. "Fear"—terror at the shaking of the very foundations—what Edna and Harry felt that night in their living

---

5. Aristotle, *Poetics*, trans. Gerald F. Else (Ann Arbor: University of Michigan Press, 1970), p. 25. Professor Else has translated *pathématôn*, usually rendered "feelings," as "tragic acts," taking it to be the plural form of the technical term pathos.

6. Cf. Walter Ong, *The Presence of the Word* (New York: Clarion Books, 1970), esp. pp. 1–16 and 111 ff.

room in Albee's *A Delicate Balance*, a sense of metaphysical horror, that sent them packing to the home of their friends Agnes and Tobias. "Purification"—catharsis or cleansing, the end of the convulsion, victory over the fever, renewal of life and hope.

There is a footnote on "fear" in Professor Sewall's book when he answers the question of what tragedy means to be: "It recalls the original terror, harking back to a world that antedates the conceptions of philosophy, the consolations of the later religions, and whatever constructions the human mind has devised to persuade itself that its universe is secure. It recalls the original un-reason, the terror of the irrational. It sees man as questioner, naked, unaccommodated, alone, facing mysterious, demonic forces in his own nature and outside, and the irreducible facts of suffering and death."[7] The fear is of an ontological character, having to do with a refacing of man's entire relationship to his cosmos. As Professor Knox put it in his admirable essay on *Oedipus the King*, "Sophocles' *Oedipus* is not only the greatest creation of a major poet and the classic representative figure of his age: he is also one of the long series of tragic protagonists who stand as symbols of human aspiration and despair before the characteristic dilemma of Western civilization—the problem of man's true nature, his proper place in the universe."[8] It is the addressing again of this problem, in the light of the impact made on traditional solutions by developments in social, psychological, and cosmological thought, that is the perennial task of tragedy. Indeed, man cannot come to terms with his own developments until tragedy has chastened his spirit and satisfied the Faustian enigma of his being. Until then, he exists in guilty tension with the achievements of his own mind and spirit, awaiting the punishment meted out to Prometheus or Faust.

7. Sewall, *Vision of Tragedy*, pp. 4–5.
8. Bernard Knox, "Sophocles' Oedipus," *Tragic Themes in Western Literature*, ed. Cleanth Brooks (New Haven: Yale University Press, 1955), p. 7.

This is seen rather clearly in *Oedipus*. There is a plague upon the city-state of Thebes, symbolizing the skewedness of the times. The priest implores Oedipus to show himself as he was when he solved the riddle of the Sphinx and to save the city again. There is a veiled rebuke in his words, for Oedipus is not the same as he was; he has begun to think of himself as a kind of god. The priest calls him *tyrannos*—not king, but tyrant—one who acceded to the throne by seizing power. Only later, immediately after Oedipus realizes that he is the son and killer of Laius, and has married his own mother, does the chorus call him king. Ironically he has been king all along, but has not known it.

A further irony is couched in Oedipus' very name. *Oida*, he says too frequently—"I know." And he doesn't know. But there is another word very near to *oida* in the way it sounds —*oidi*, "swell." He is *oidi-pous*—"swollen foot"—the man with the clubfoot. While he thinks he knows, but doesn't, the poet stabs him again and again in the play by a recurrent use of the word *pous*, or "foot," a reminder he seems not to recognize. Swollen in knowledge, he cannot see that he must at last be tripped up by what Sophocles called the "high-footed" laws of Zeus. He will not listen to Tiresias, the blind man who can "see," who prophesies unerringly the outcome of the play; therefore, when it is over, when the swollen one is deflated, and shown his sin, it is proper that he accept blindness himself and become an outcast. He has been out of step, has gone against nature, without knowing it. He is not an evil man; on the contrary, he has been a good ruler. But he lacked humility; he has never conceived of himself as a criminal; he has never considered that he might be out of phase with the cosmos.

From a certain viewpoint, it can be almost staggering to think of this play's being presented to a Periclean audience flanking the cultic priests and the sacrificial altar. They had every reason for pride. They were sophisticated, talented, expert in the arts and politics. Their times were so lustrous

that succeeding generations would remember them as a
golden age. Protagoras could understandably proclaim that
man is the measure of all things. But guilt dogged their progress. They had transformed theology and culture, reordering
existence. However certain their time may look to ours, it was
in reality a time of confusion and fear and uncertainty. Oedipus, the enlightened king, became their lightning rod. He
did not die at the end of the play—his mother did—but he
was severely humbled. And the audience was reminded that
though man may seize power, in any generation, he is still
finite, still circumscribed by deities and destinies, still at the
mercy of the times, which, in their own way, are inexorably
moral. No, they were more than reminded. They *participated*
in the experience of Oedipus. Their *oida* gave way to *oidi*
which in turn became *oida* again: from knowledge to obtuseness to deeper knowledge. They were cleansed with the
protagonist.

Walter Stein, in *Criticism as Dialogue*, focuses on a similar
kind of reversal which he sees at the heart of Shakespeare's
tragedies. In *Lear*, for instance, we confront again man's essential pride and blindness of spirit, which, when revelation
or illumination occurs, is turned to humility and actual
blindness.

The context for Elizabethan drama, we recall, was not unlike that of Sophocles. The times were riven to the depths by
the tensions between old and new, Roman and Protestant,
orthodox and heretical. It had been a scant hundred years
since Henry had declared himself head of the church in England, fifty since Elizabeth had secured Protestantism in the
realm. The Middle Ages were by no means dead. Superstitions and medievalisms persisted side by side with the latest
cosmological and theological opinions. Men were intoxicated
by the headiness of the new science and the new learning, yet
felt the abyss opening under their feet. *Hamlet* and *Lear* were
dangerous liturgies, accomplishing what they did as tragedies
because they represented such risks of the human spirit.

What Professor Stein is most interested in is the sense of joy which I. A. Richards first noted as standing so strangely central to the transaction in *Lear*. Why should a play which deals in such fundamental horror, systematically and resolutely destroying an old man's understanding of himself and the world, finally contain such joy? From Richard's point of view, it shouldn't. "Tragedy is only possible to a mind which is for the moment agnostic or Manichean," he said. "The least touch of any theology which has a compensating Heaven to offer a tragic hero is fatal."[9] Therefore the sense of joy is strange and mysterious; it seems to appear for no obvious reason.

But precisely because the joy is real and there is no obvious reason for it, Stein concludes that it must be "the index of some sort of real, relevant apprehension" and not merely "a marvelous psychological trick." He proceeds to dissect the play, not so much to uncover the presence of joy in the dismembered pieces as to see how the pieces themselves are finally transcended by its presence, to find out what are the reasons of the heart which ultimately refuse to surrender to the cumulative logic of despair. The apparent invincibility of the despair is integral to the genius of the play. Other tragedies may engulf us in desperateness, says Stein, but Lear goes further, strangling hope after hope and value after value until it finally annihilates all hope with: "*Enter* LEAR, *with* CORDELIA *dead in his arms.*" This is why we have the Fool—not for mere comic relief, but to render the despair more total. "The Fool is there to ensure that every conceivable alternative to despair shall be given its chance, and then slain."[10]

The mock-suicide scene, Edgar's leading the blinded Gloucester over a very shallow "cliff," becomes, in this context,

9. I. A. Richards, *Principles of Literary Criticism* (New York: Harcourt, Brace, 1948), p. 246.
10. Walter Stein, *Criticism as Dialogue* (Cambridge: Cambridge University Press, 1969), p. 107.

much more than a cruelly gratuitous act. As Stein says, it "embraces much more than Gloucester's personal experience," and also "stands proxy for Lear's—who has been physically absent since the Fool's liquidation, and is presently to reappear at his most lunatic and most profound."[11] In fact, it "distils the entire tragic rhythm of the play." It not only compresses the movement from despair to acceptance, but *interprets* the larger movement of the play. Gloucester is finally able to assent to Edgar's assurance that "Thy life's a miracle" and, in his blindness, to see things *feelingly*, as he later puts it to Lear. The symbolic resolution is arrived at:

> henceforth I'll bear
> Affliction till it do cry out itself
> "Enough, enough," and die.

The apparent gratuitousness of the scene is then in fact "the tragic surpassing of cruelty: tragedy pushed beyond mere tragic outrage. If it is 'cruel,' it is cruel only as *Job* is cruel (since the facts of tragic experience are cruel). If affliction *must* be borne—and the play makes *us* see that it must—the world ceases to be bottomlessly absurd."[12] The characters and the audience receive a kind of cosmic apprehension, an insight into existence, which assures them of ultimate meaning in the universe, and even in suffering and death, and which makes sense of Lear's last speech to Cordelia:

> Upon such sacrifices, my Cordelia,
> The gods themselves throw incense.

It makes sense, as Stein observes, not merely by confronting us with the worst and enabling us to withstand, but by finally abandoning us to a conclusion in which the worst has the last word and *still* enabling us to withstand. "The world remains what it was, a merciless, heartbreaking world. Lear is broken

11. Ibid., p. 108.
12. Ibid., p. 110.

by it, but he has learned to love and be loved; to gaze at the maddening cosmos through radical, 'foolish' love."[13]

When we think thus of joy extruded from horror, we are reminded also of the novels of Dostoevsky, which depend for their quintessential quality on this same willingness to view the insanity of the human situation with love and forgiveness. What strikes us at once about Dostoevsky, says the Russian poet Vyacheslav Ivanov, is the way his stories approximate the form of tragedy. It is not as if he had deliberately striven for the approximation; on the contrary, he hit upon it only by accident and in all innocence. It was simply that his whole being demanded it. "The inner structure of his creative genius was tragic."[14] In his works we are confronted at every moment with an event which is not merely what it is in itself but which becomes a microcosm of an entire tragic universe. "It is as if we saw the tragedy through a magnifying-glass, and found in its cell-structure a repetition and emphasis of the same principle of antinomy that informs the whole organism."[15]

Dostoevsky's secret, apparently learned in a narrow escape from execution and in his Siberian exile, was to view the world compassionately. The world was going mad. He felt that, saw it, dreamed it, shuddered at it. *The Possessed,* with its title drawn from the image of the demoniac's devil-ridden swine, was the picture of it: men rushing headlong to their doom, and no way to stop themselves. Atheism and anarchy were convulsing everything. Men breathed crime in the very air around them. Suffering—*great* suffering—was inevitable. And yet, at the heart of the anguish, like the calm eye of a storm, there is also that sense of mystery, that miracle of joy.

The paradigm is in *The Brothers Karamazov,* when Dmitri is being tried for the murder of his father, which he did not

13. Ibid., p. 113.
14. Vyacheslav Ivanov, *Freedom and the Tragic Life,* trans. Norman Cameron (New York: Noonday Press, 1960), p. 7.
15. Ibid., p. 11.

actually commit even though, as Ivan points out in the court-
room, every man desires the death of his male parent. He is
asleep on a bench and has a dream. Sweeping across the frozen
steppes in a sleigh, he comes upon a village that has been
burned out. The refugees are standing on the outskirts of the
town, their arms and hands outstretched in need. His eye
fastens upon a baby in its mother's arms; it is blue from the
cold. The dream is enough. When he awakens, Dmitri is prepared to accept his fate. He is ready to go to Siberia for a
crime that was not his because it was humanity's crime and
he has found humanity. He and the refugees from the village,
he and the babe in the cold, he and the true murderer, are
one. The impact of such an insight is staggering on him; it
transforms him. And the sign, the symbolic benediction,
when he awakens is the fact that some nameless person, or
an angel, has placed a pillow under his head while he slept.
He is ecstatic at the discovery of this. The years in exile
mean nothing. He will go there and keep the name of
God alive in the prisons, where it is always most alive. The
catharsis (for that is what it is) has occurred, and with it a
deep sense of the joy of being human.

This mode of seeing, which Dostoevsky regarded as the
only antithesis to the world's deep and brooding chaos, he
called *proniknovenie*, "intuitive seeing through" or "spiritual
penetration." Its result, when it occurs in a character, is
always transvaluation, but transvaluation limited to the character himself. He alone is able to see the world with new
understanding, for the understanding is always an act of faith.
It cannot be "proven" either rationally or by a consensus of
opinion. Its only reasons, in other words, are, like Shakespeare's, reasons of the heart.

This then is the pattern of tragedy, established in at least
three points across a number of centuries. Despite all his
knowledge and cleverness, man gets askew of the universe,
and crimes occur. The result of skewedness is anguish. The
answer to anguish is humiliation, being brought down to the

earth again, to the *humis*, and chastened into a new acceptance of life. And the result of humiliation and acceptance is
a feeling of joy, of inexplicable comfort about the universe
and one's relationship to it, of *belonging*, of peace and rest.
Suffering deepens the consciousness of man until, like Job,
he sees with the eye what he had previously only heard of
with his ears. Out at the naked edge of the world, staring into
the abyss and yearning to die, he discovers what it means to
live.

In the beginning we spoke of God and suffering, and of
"undeserved suffering," as inevitable constituents of tragedy.
Dame Helen, in *Religion and Literature*, refers to the Hebrew doctrine of the creation of the world as "a tremendous
leap of the human imagination," and suggests that the concept of a responsible Creator has heightened tragic potentiali-
ties even beyond what they were for the Greeks.[10]

Whether that is so or not, we are faced today, in the wake
of Freud and the modern philosophers, with the problem of
the desacralization of the universe. What happens to tragedy
when God has been displaced from the heavens and suffering
has been psychologized? Can one then even speak of "undeserved suffering"? Must not the "skewedness" to which we
have referred exist only in the mind of the protagonist, and
is it not possible through psychoanalysis to restore him to
harmony with his cosmos without treating of crime and
criminality at all? His cosmos is in fact only his own soul or
personality, and not a universal cosmos. Drama is thus reduced to psychodrama, and its liturgical proportions are
shrunken to an interiority immediately defying Aristotle's
definition of tragedy as an imitation of "an action which has
serious implications, is complete, and possesses magnitude."

The *tragedification* of the universe, says the *chosiste* writer
Alain Robbe-Grillet, is man's attempt, through metaphor, to

16. Gardner, *Religion and Literature*, pp. 55–60.

have the universe, to engulf it, to possess it, to subsume it, to make it capable of solidarity with himself. Without the sense of solidarity, he feels that he lives in a void; nothing coheres; he experiences the chill of loneliness; so he personifies the universe, prostrates himself before it, and affects a reunion or reestablishment of relation.

> Let us retrace, as an example, the functioning of "solitude." I call out. No one answers me. Instead of concluding that there is no one there—which could be a pure and simple observation, dated and localized in space and time—I decide to act as if there were someone there, but someone who, for one reason or another, will not answer. The silence which follows my outcry is henceforth no longer a *true* silence; it is charged with a content, a meaning, a depth, a soul—which immediately sends me back to my own. The distance between my cry, to my own ears, and the mute (perhaps deaf) interlocutor to whom it is addressed becomes an anguish, my hope and my despair, a meaning in my life. Henceforth nothing will matter except this false void and the problems it raises for me. Should I call any longer? Should I shout louder? Should I utter different words? I try once again. . . . Very quickly I realize that no one will answer; but the invisible presence I continue to create by my call obliges me to hurl my wretched cries into the silence forever. Soon the sound they make begins to stupefy me. As though bewitched, I call again . . . and again. My solitude, aggravated, is ultimately transmuted into a superior necessity for my alienated consciousness, a promise of my redemption. And I am obliged, if this redemption is to be fulfilled, to persist until my death, crying out for nothing.[17]

The world man perceives then, says Robbe-Grillet, is only a fabricated world, for he has extinguished the possibility of knowing the real one. "Drowned in the *depth* of things, man ultimately no longer even perceives them: his role is soon limited to experiencing, in their name, totally *humanized* impressions and desires."[18] Things, posited from the start as

---

17. Alain Robbe-Grillet, *For a New Novel: Essays on Fiction*, trans. Richard Howard (New York: Grove Press, 1965), p. 60.
18. Ibid., p. 68.

not being man, "remain constantly out of reach and are, ultimately, neither comprehended in a natural alliance nor recovered by suffering."[19] Man's sickness is thus self-perpetuating and cannot be cured until the humanization or tragedification process is broken. For the present man is conditioned by the process—even Robbe-Grillet himself—but he foresees a day when man will have freed himself from it.

What we have had and are having in the interim is works of literature which express what Professor Murray Krieger calls "the tragic vision" without the sense of epiphany or completion of the act of purification which marked the formal tragedy. The tragic vision was born inside tragedy, says Krieger, as part of it, but has become separated from the form which bore the palliative and is therefore inconsolable.[20] It is perhaps logical to expect that the only development now capable of relieving the vision is the attainment of a new level of nonexpectancy such as Robbe-Grillet describes, where the ambiguity or double nature of characters is dropped and man no longer looks for any *meaning* in things or events.

Much of the writing in the vein of the tragic vision has taken the form of metaphysical rebellion or Prometheanism. A large measure of the tension and conflict which we find unresolved in the works of such figures as Melville, Eliot, Hardy, Lautréamont, Baudelaire, Dreiser, Hemingway, Camus, and Malamud derives from the fact that they occupy an era of transition between one tacitly acknowledged world-view and another. They are the anguished psalmists of the twilight, hymning the death of Christendom's God. They may still desire solidarity with the earth or the cosmos or some super-mythic unity, but they are unwilling that it should suffer the benediction of the Christian religion.

Even as deniers of God, interestingly, these writers provide us with haunting remembrances of the holy—so much so that

19. Ibid., p. 70.
20. Murray Krieger, *The Tragic Vision: Variations on a Theme in Literary Interpretation* (Chicago: University of Chicago Press, 1966), pp. 2–4.

many readers profess to find a more compelling case for theism, or at least a stronger sense of the numinous, in them than in avowedly religious authors. As Rudolf Otto has reminded us, blasphemy itself is often more evocative of the transcendent than piety and obedience are.[21] Religious folkways, language, and rituals are constantly becoming idolatrous, and the act of desecrating the idols temporarily educes a renewed sense of the spiritual. And even though this sense may seem more demonic than affirmative, because it proceeds from an act of violation, it tends at least momentarily to revalidate theism as an ontological reality.

This is true, for example, in *Moby-Dick*, where, if we are able to follow at all Lawrance Thompson's argument in *Melville's Quarrel with God*, the deep-scarred Captain Ahab, subtly and malignantly damned, is drawn to his doom not merely by a phenomenal whale but by an utterly fascinating symbol of the Calvinistic God himself, plunging, sounding, and creating great vortices of danger and death in the spirit world. The inevitable feeling of mystery and transcendence in the story rises out of the sense of forbiddenness and desecration we experience as the *Pequod* is driven—plunged—deeper and deeper into the inner sanctum of the whale's presence. The imagery which describes the intensity of danger in the whale's vicinity is unmistakably and ingeniously religious.[22] We know, though it is never explicitly stated, that Ahab is bent upon entering the Holy of Holies and engaging there with the strange, supernal monster which has maimed or castrated him and which he has vowed to love.

Professor Scott, in his essay on "The Tragic Vision and the Christian Faith," does not hesitate to call *Moby-Dick* a tragedy.[23] But we must entertain some doubt, it seems to me, as

21. Rudolf Otto, *The Idea of the Holy* (New York: Oxford University Press, 1957), pp. 61–65.
22. For more explicit reference, see the author's *The Failure of Theology in Modern Literature* (Nashville: Abingdon Press, 1963), pp. 127–32.
23. Nathan A. Scott, Jr., *The Broken Center: Studies in the Theological Horizon of Modern Literature* (New Haven: Yale University Press, 1966), pp. 119–44.

to whether any catharsis or spiritual insight ever occurs in the narrative, or, if it does, whether it occurs to the protagonist himself. Ahab dies essentially unrepentant and thirsty for vengeance. Had he survived instead of Ishmael, and gone humbly through the world like Coleridge's mariner, narrating his tale of a chastening in the deep, there might have been a kind of catharsis. Or perhaps we can speak of a unique kind of tragic structure in *Moby-Dick*, whereby the stance of prideful rebellion and the stance of chastened intelligence, normally combined in the single protagonist, are here occupied by two different characters, Ahab and Ishmael, so that we read the story as a tragedy only when we regard it binocularly or stereoptically. It is finally difficult to say whether or not Melville intended the book to be a singular epic of resistance, without the amelioration of a cathartic viewpoint, and this difficulty is only intensified by the ironic complexities of *Billy Budd, Foretopman* and the apparently unnegotiable antinomies raised by the various critics of that little narrative. But we begin, in this transitional era of Prometheanism or rebellion, to face a new and absorbing problem, namely, how to defy the gods without ending in utter nihilism, or, as Camus phrased it, how to say no without implying a renunciation,[24] and this problem places an unusual strain on the whole question of the nature and meaning of tragedy.

Consider the case of a more recent expression of the tragic vision, Bernard Malamud's novel *The Fixer*. In some ways this novel is as Dostoevskian as any of our period. Yet it lacks the specific *proniknovenie* or moment of redemption so characteristic of the Russian's greatest novels. Yakov Bok, the mendicant Jewish tinkerer, leads a life of excruciating loneliness—a loneliness as metaphysical as it is physical, for he is a death-of-God Jew. The God of his fathers, he is convinced, has never been more than an invention for comforting a people almost continuously in exile. The sight of his departure

24. Albert Camus, *The Rebel* (New York: Vintage Books, 1956), p. 13.

for Kiev after his wife has deserted him and he has said
goodbye to his father-in-law is unforgettable: a starkly lonely
man, down on his luck, rolling slowly along over the cold,
darkening horizons of the Russian landscape, cursing God,
his wife, the world, and his horse. Surely things will improve
in Kiev. But they do not; on the contrary, they get worse. A
child is killed, apparently in a savage, ritualistic kind of murder, and the government, wishing to initiate a new series of
pogroms against the Jews, ties the death to Bok, who had indeed once chased the child away from the brickyard where
he worked. Bok is imprisoned and urged to confess. He is
treated with nearly unbearable brutality—starved, beaten,
badgered, neglected—yet resolutely refuses to succumb. His
incredible history of suffering bleakly dramatizes the absence
of justice in the world, and perhaps even accuses the idea of
a God who would permit one of his chosen ones to languish
so. But there is no denouement to the story. Bok is about to
have a hearing, after months and months of imprisonment,
and is on his way to the hearing when his carriage is mobbed
by the angry populace. *Finis.*

Again, as in *Moby-Dick*, there is no self-evident catharsis.
We suspect that the author did not wish us to have one, that
he did not wish to be put off that easily. The novel is an
indictment of the world's inhumanity; and a catharsis would
answer the indictment. We are left with a disturbing tale,
unrelieved and unmitigated in its bitterness. Bok is a pathetic
figure. As a character, he is hauntingly real. We can see the
hairs on his neck, the dirt in his fingernails, the slow, rhyth-
mical movement of his breast as he inhales and exhales. We
feel his depression, his weariness, his isolation. We also feel
his strength of character, his tenacity, his pride, his stubborn-
ness. There is something glorious about him, even in abject-
ness. He is, almost, a truly tragic figure. Only there is no
catharsis. We are out at the edge of the abyss with him, naked
and alone, but the epiphany doesn't come. We wait for it, but
it does not appear. Why? What is wrong? It would be unfair

to Malamud to insist that it should appear in this book; he evidently did not design such an appearance. But the fact that we keep waiting for an epiphany, or some kind of relief or breakthrough, is worth noting. We expect one when the conditions observed in this novel have been fulfilled. We have been disciplined by the traditions of tragic literature to believe, when man is stripped down and appears before us so real and true, that then some evidence of the deity, or at least of some metaphysical unity behind existence, will likewise break into view. We find it difficult to believe in man precisely as Malamud has shown him to us, resolute and unyielding and with an outraged sense of justice, without also believing in the Hebraic tradition—the tradition of Job—which molded such a man and made his presence here before us possible. Such a man, in such extremities, *implies* God.

But no, Camus would answer, that does not follow. According to the old logic such a man might have implied God, but now we must leave the facts where they are and, in so doing, compel ourselves to rethink the question of God. This may not be a time for submission—not, at any rate, to a version of transcendence somehow incompatible with the way we understand history and the self. We may presently be forced into new conceptions of the transcendent, for the metaphysical rebel actually defies more than he denies; but for the moment we must refuse to lie about our feelings.

The example of Camus himself is instructive. It is impossible to overstate his indebtedness to Dostoevsky; in some ways he never worked his way out of the shadow cast by the Russian. His preoccupation with human suffering and his enormous concern for the earth and how man is dependent on it were both first learned from Dostoevsky. But he could never accept the theistic assumptions of Dostoevsky's writings, and consequently never quite attained their heights of resignation and mystical joy. It is my guess that this is also the reason we do not find in his works the demonic intensity found so often in Dostoevsky: when the peaks of metaphysical acceptance are truncated, the valleys no longer seem so deep.

What Camus appears to have been seeking was a mode of identifying transcendent joy without necessarily endorsing former theologies and world-views of transcendence. "Secret of my universe," he wrote in his diary, "imagining God without human immortality."[25] He wished to preserve the kind of spiritual penetration he had found in Dostoevsky without attempting to keep alive a traditional understanding of God and the universe. Thus Meursault in *The Stranger* persistently and pointedly rejects the approach of the chaplain, whose entreaty is for a capitulation not unlike that of Dmitri in *The Brothers Karamazov.* He does not desire God and salvation, he declares; he desires a blond-headed girl whom he knows, and he desires to go on living; that is all. In fact, he says, he could live for a thousand years immured in the trunk of an old tree, if only he could gaze at the blue sky every day. We may quibble at calling this "transcendent joy" because it seems so different at first from the religious resignation in the classical tradition of tragic literature. But if it is examined more sympathetically the difference may be much smaller than we thought. There is in fact a penetration in *The Stranger* (which has not gone unnoticed by Robbe-Grillet[26]), a recognition of the unity of the cosmos, signalized by a number of things—by Meursault's acceptance of the unjust verdict, by his fascination and identification with the newspaper clipping about the Czech murder story, by his affirmation of life in a cell, and by his reverie about his mother and approval of the way she found new life in her declining years. It would have been a falsification of Camus's way of looking at human existence for him to have surrendered to a more stylized, Christian interpretation of life. By holding the anguish where it was and refusing to relinquish it, as he felt that Kierkegaard did, he forced it to *remain*

25. Albert Camus, *Notebooks 1942–1951*, trans. Justin O'Brien (New York: Alfred A. Knopf, 1965), p. 12.
26. Robbe-Grillet, *For a New Novel*, pp. 62–64.

metaphysical, and in turn compelled us, because we are innately satisfied with the justice of Meursault's position, to reexamine the nature of God and his relationship to time and the universe. This is the immense but deceptively simple achievement of *The Stranger*, and the seldom recognized secret of the attraction which draws us back again and again to the little novel. We can never dismiss it, because it defines so lucidly the watershed in recent theological development.

Having said this, we can return in point of time to the novels of Kafka and ask whether the same was not also true of them, that they too record subtly disguised, barely recognizable epiphanies, which make of them, for all their interiority, at least demitragedies. If *The Trial* may be said to be "about" anything in particular, it is about Joseph K.'s struggle with his pride and the ultimate resolution of that struggle. K. is "stiff-necked," like Oedipus and Lear; he cannot believe he is guilty of anything. When offered Titorelli's interpretation of his three alternatives—ostensible acquittal, indefinite postponement, and definite acquittal—he refuses to accept anything but definite acquittal. He mounts an attack upon the entire legal system and the traditions of his fathers in an attempt to convert the whole situation and bring the system and the traditions to their knees before him as a solitary individual. The housekeeper sees through him when she says she thinks he wants to change things. In the end, of course, K. is hustled out of town by a couple of Laurel-and-Hardy figures who argue over who is to execute him and finally slay him "like a dog." At one level of interpretation, the individual has been arraigned and sentenced and annihilated by society with all its conventions, mores, and indifference to the person. But there is another level, inspired by clues which Kafka was careful to place, which concludes that K. not only concurred in the decision but actually wished his death. He did, as a matter of fact, reject the possibility of indefinite postponement of his case, and, when there appeared to be a possibility of intervention on the way to the execution, he clutched the arms of his custodians and hurried them along to avoid it. There is, in other words, a form of insight or acceptance suggestive of, if not actually tantamount to, the moment of catharsis in traditional tragic literature.

There is a similar acceptance in *The Castle*. K. has been distraught about having his surveyor's appointment validated by the lord of the castle. He has continually insisted upon his right to see the lord, to have a direct access that no one except perhaps the highest officials of the village have. Getting to the lord has become an obsession with him, interfering with his ability to live normally and happily like other persons. But he finally realizes, as he watches Pepi struggling to ingratiate herself with Klamm, that the answer is in acceptance instead of struggle. "When I compare myself with you," he says to Pepi,

> something of this kind dawns on me: it is as if we had both striven too intensely, too noisily, too childishly, with too little experience, to get something that for instance with Frieda's calm and Frieda's matter-of-factness can be got easily and without much ado. We have tried to get it by crying, by scratching, by tugging—just as a child tugs at the tablecloth, gaining nothing, but only bringing all the splendid things down on the floor and putting them out of its reach forever.[27]

Max Brod said, in the German edition of *The Castle*, that Kafka had conceived of an ending in which K. would lie dying in his bed, surrounded by townspeople, when he received a message from the castle that, while he had no right to be there, he might remain and work there.

Kafka's persistent theme, in other words, was the same as Sophocles' or Shakespeare's or Dostoevsky's or Camus's—the problem of man's true nature and of his proper place in the universe. And the resolution of the problem was essentially the same: man must somehow get beyond his stubborn, blind-

27. Franz Kafka, *The Castle*, trans. Willa and Edwin Muir (New York: Alfred A. Knopf, 1964), pp. 404–5.

ing pride and willingly submit to the unity of all things, accepting even evil and injustice as an integral part of cosmic existence. The difference in his approach, as in Camus's after him, and perhaps Beckett's, was primarily in terms of *locus*. The older, traditional form of tragedy operated simultaneously from two *loci*, one external and one internal. Events in the cosmos paralleled events in the psyche, and part of the author's business or technique was to reveal the interplay between the two realms. In Kafka and certain writers who succeeded him, the *loci* became fused, or else so much emphasis was laid on the psychic *locus* that the external *locus* became vague and uncertain, and appeared at times to be a relatively unimportant extension of the inner *locus*.

This "tragic split" between the psyche and the cosmos is not entirely new to our time, of course; it was certainly manifest as early as the plays of Shakespeare. But the Freudian revolution of the last half-century appears to have validated and thus accelerated a stronger and stronger emphasis on the psyche. As Joseph Campbell says in *The Hero with a Thousand Faces*, the hero-deed to be wrought today is not what it once was, when the wilderness lay outside of the individual, when there were tigers and tribes to be slain and plagues to be quelled. The crucial mystery no longer lies in the plant and animal world, or even in the miracle of the spheres; it is in man himself. "The modern hero-deed must be that of questing to bring to light again the lost Atlantis of the coordinated soul."[28]

I mentioned Beckett. Some word must be said about his work, which probably, when histories of the stage are written, will be judged to stand nearer the caliber of Shakespeare's than any the postwar years have produced. It would be hard to imagine a world further from Shakespeare's than Beckett's. Bloodless, colorless, dry, broken, effete—it is like the sands of New Mexico after a nuclear blast. It has been "stripped," to

28. Joseph Campbell, *The Hero with a Thousand Faces* (New York: Meridian Books, 1967), p. 388.

use Father William Lynch's word for it, denuded to the point
where the artist must begin with failure and try to make
something of that.[29] Beckett is too classically trained, too
much steeped in the great traditions, finally to reach what the
Marxist critic Roland Barthes has called *le degré zéro*, at
which all vestiges of humanity have been annihilated, but he
does press his characters in that direction, and that is one of
the fascinating things about his books and plays. It is like a
game in which one sees how close he can come to the edge of
the abyss without really going over. It is James Joyce forced
through a keyhole, through a pinpoint, through the narrow-
est isthmus conceivable; and the more Beckett does it the
narrower he appears to be able to construct the isthmus.
Murphy, Molloy, Malone Dies, The Unnamable—with each
of the novels, especially, there is a tightening of the aperture,
a gradual narrowing, so that the reader says it is impossible
to reduce human consciousness any more, and so that, reading *The Unnamable*, he *swears* that it is impossible to go
further.

The play *Endgame*, then, is really a caricature of this re-
ductionary process. Four characters hold the stage against the
end of the world. One is an invalid in a wheelchair who, at
the beginning and end of the play, sits with a nasty, blood-
stained handkerchief spread over his face. Another, somewhat
younger than the invalid but still by no means in the bloom
of youth, has a peculiar disease and cannot sit down. And
there are two nauseatingly senile characters, the "accursed
progenitors" of the invalid, who live like tired Jack-in-the-
boxes in dust bins at the side of the stage, eating, drinking,
urinating, defecating, whining, remonstrating, reminiscing,
forgetting, all without ever leaving the confinement of the
bins. These are the last pieces on the chess board. The game
is nearly over.

As Richard Coe has pointed out, the controlling motif in

29. William F. Lynch, *Christ and Prometheus: A New Image of the Secular*
(Notre Dame: University of Notre Dame Press, 1970), pp. 67–68.

all Beckett's writings is the one hinted at in the opening speech of *Endgame:* "Finished, it's nearly finished, nearly finished, it must be nearly finished. Grain upon grain, one by one, and one day, suddenly, there's a heap, a little heap, the impossible heap."[30] The reference is to Zeno's analogy of the millet heap, and the impossibility, if one transferred half of the heap into another heap, and half again, and half again, and so on without stopping, of ever exhausting the original heap. Beckett's characters are clearly diminished from the former grandeur of man, almost to the point of being unrecognizable.[31] But they *are* recognizable, and must continue to be, for the human image is finally ineffaceable.

This is likewise the answer to the riddle of Beckett's religious position, which always seems, after a performance of a play like *Waiting for Godot,* so eminently arguable. Yes, Beckett is an agnostic, but not quite. Yes, he is an atheist, but not quite. He is always approaching zero on this matter, just as he is on the matter of humanity, but, for the very reason that he cannot quite push humanity over the verge, he cannot finally extinguish the infinitesimal residue of faith and hope. Vladimir and Estragon never see Godot, or never know if they have seen him, but they cannot stop waiting. The invalid in the *Endgame* may call the others to prayer, sit there with head bowed in silence, and then interrupt all of them with the line, "The bastard . . . he doesn't exist!" but he and his perpendicular associate cannot give up the feeling that something is alive out there in the desert, something like a louse or a rodent or a child, something christological and messianic, that will get things started all over again. What is left of man as he has been known supposes also something left of God as he has been known.

There are interesting parallels or similarities in Beckett to the line of Western tragic literature. He makes the point that

---

30. Richard Coe, *Samuel Beckett* (New York: Grove Press, 1964), pp. 88–89.
31. Hugh Kenner (*Samuel Beckett: A Critical Study* [New York: Grove Press, 1961], p. 67) thinks the man in the wheelchair, who is named Hamm, is the descendant of Shakespeare's Hamlet.

was made in Job and Aeschylus and Sophocles and Shakespeare, that man cannot die when he chooses, cannot opt out
of his anguish, but must bear it out to the bitter end. Vladimir and Estragon cannot hang themselves, nor the world-
weary characters of *Endgame* precipitate a conclusion to their
sad state of affairs, any more than Oedipus could terminate
everything by suicide when he discovered the nature of his
imbroglio. The difference is that Beckett plays everything out
in the last backwash of the tragic situation, where action is
all but impossible and suffering must be endured in the most
abject stolidity. As one critic said of *Waiting for Godot*, which
has two acts, it is a play in which "nothing happens—twice."
The millet heap is too small for action on the old scale. Only
the last tremors, the dying reverberations of actions, are
experienced now.

Beckett's personae still discover themselves and the gods in
the consequences of tragic action. But because the action is
so utterly reduced in scope, because the tired pendulum is
nearly at a standstill, the discovered selves are only shadows
of their former selves, and the vitality of the gods is diminished in proportion. I have elaborated elsewhere on the thesis
that various parts of the Mass, fragmentary, disarranged, illusory, are hidden throughout *Waiting for Godot*, so that the
play occurs in the stylized but submerged form of a ritual.[32]
Yet the characters cannot be said to be aware that this is so.
They are so vague, so listless, so worn out with it all, that
they can no longer recognize and cause to cohere the presence
of God in their midst.

I use those words "cause to cohere" with serious intention,
for I think that Beckett, superb artist and cunning thinker
that he is, draws the theme of the disappearing or evaporat-
ing God precisely in terms of the metaphysical boredom of
man. I cannot recall a place in all of Beckett's works where

32. Cf. *World in Collapse: The Vision of Absurd Drama* (New York: Dell
Publishing Co., 1971), pp. 21–23; also elaborated slightly in the following
chapter in this book.

God himself is directly impugned or denied; even the expletive in *Endgame*, "The bastard . . . he doesn't exist," is more
an indictment of the characters and their wizened sensibilities
than it is of the deity. There is, in fact, an almost indefineable
sense of grace behind the facade of Beckett's world. He smiles,
and makes the texture of his works ripple (ever so slightly)
with mirth and humor, despite the fact that he looks out on
emptiness and nothingness. It is as if he knew he was myopic,
that there was something he could not see, and that that
something, at depths beyond visibility to others, sustained
him for seeing the satisfyingly humorous side of man's desic-
cation and obscenity more closely at hand.

What of tragedy and the post-"Godotian" theater? Perhaps
the answer is summarized in Tom Stoppard's clever play
Rosencrantz and Guildenstern Are Dead, which is only um-
bilically related to Shakespeare (Ros and Guil were the two
courtiers assigned to watch over Hamlet in his melancholia)
and stands poles apart from traditional notions of the tragic.
There is not really any plot in the play, any more than there
was in *Godot*; inaction, not action, is the order—or disorder—
of the day. There is great concern for the sense of illusion
which invades all of life today, vitiating the possibility of
meaningful behavior. Everything is psychologized into quies-
cence. Guil recalls Chuang Tzu's story of the man who fell
asleep and dreamed he was a butterfly, and, upon awakening,
did not know whether he was a man who dreamed he was a
butterfly or a butterfly yet dreaming he was a man. And he
adds a splendid little parable of his own about a man who
thought he saw a unicorn crossing the road ahead of him and
was excited about it until other people reported the same
phenomenon; then he became phlegmatic about it, because
the commonness of the vision had made it "as thin as reality."
In this ricochet world of illusion-reality, death itself, the final
reality in Elizabethan drama, is retrograded to the point of
boredom. It is not, Guil instructs the court players, something
which can really be seen happening, "gasps and blood and

falling about"; it is "just a man failing to reappear, that's all." And God, in this affectively truncated existence, cannot hope to be given any more pledge of reality than human suffering; he is reduced, when all is said and done, to "the single assumption which makes our existence viable—that somebody is *watching*"—but that assumption is actually more than the personae of this play can offer.

Is this the end of the line? Must the tragic vision end finally in a *reductio ad absurdum*, in what Erich Kahler in *The Tower and the Abyss* calls "ahumanity," the last twist of the dehumanization process? Not that the genre of absurd literature is not instructive to the human spirit in its own way—we shall deal with this in the following chapter. But has the universe become so flat and sterile, so one-dimensional, that it is no longer possible or even desirable to evoke feelings of transcendence in the audience?

There is considerable evidence to suggest that it has. Such a deflation would help to explain why even a play like Arthur Miller's *Death of a Salesman*, which he confided he hoped was a tragedy, sent audiences away weeping, without the desired catharsis or purification. Pathos today is usually so psychologized, so linked to the neurotic conditions of human life we are all so much aware of, that it is discharged, if at all, by actions totally unheroic. The universal sickness never quite becomes evil, and the protagonist is not given the opportunity of behaving nobly or grandly in a cosmos where superhuman powers are in contention. As Dame Helen remarks about Eliot's *The Family Reunion*, "The only comment on plays concerned with the 'human predicament' is either a patronizing one, 'Poor things!'; or perhaps a mood of self-pity in which we think we are all 'poor things.' "[33] We feel pity but become desensitized to the terror. Our dramatists pinch the blooms of tragedy before they are permitted

33. Gardner, *Religion and Literature*, p. 113.

to flower, and we are kept in a province of misery without relief.

It is understandable, in such a situation, that Robbe-Grillet should call for the detragedification of literature. Man need not, he says, experience the absence of signification in his universe as a lack; the tragic point of view is merely a final invention of humanism to maintain an impossible correspondence between man and things, and should be discarded. If it is not discarded, it inhibits our control of suffering and actually helps to perpetuate suffering. "Tragedy," says Robbe-Grillet, "if it consoles us today, forbids any solider conquest tomorrow. Under the appearance of a perpetual motion, it actually petrifies the universe in a sonorous malediction. There can no longer be any question of seeking some remedy for our misfortune, once tragedy convinces us to love it."[34] It is better to enter the brave new world entirely, in other words, than to surrender communion and attempt to salvage the tragic vision.

There is justification in this viewpoint, and I am almost persuaded to accept it. Almost—but not quite. One thing gnaws on me and will not suffer me to forget it. It is the theory by which Professors Sewall and Gardner attempt to explain the conditions that provide for great tragic art. Both speak of the moments which give birth to tragedy as being connected to historical epochs of dislocated values and beliefs when man is unavoidably compelled to reexamine his place and meaning in the universe. Something happens, after a period of relative stability and orthodoxy, and the "original un-reason," as Sewall calls it, returns, converting normally well-adjusted persons into lonely, unaccommodated figures who must wrestle once more with the question of their nature and with the "irreducible facts of suffering and death." There are no longer any givens; all the ground must be taken again. Dame Helen cites Professor E. R. Dodds's *The Greeks and the Irrational*, that there was among the Athenians of the

34. Robbe-Grillet, *For a New Novel*, p. 61.

fifth century B.C. "a deepened awareness of human insecurity
and human helplessness," and points out that parallel conditions existed in sixteenth-century England.[35]

If there is really a correlation between the social and psychological unsettledness of a new era and the possibilities of
tragedy in the era, then ours is hardly a time to be despairing
of tragedy. On the contrary, conditions were never better.
The global village, as McLuhan calls it, is as fecund a birth-
ing-ground as either fifth-century Athens or sixteenth-century
London ever dreamed of being. The disturbance in all our
systems—in theology, in the arts, in the body politic, in the
understanding of man—is the profoundest men have ever
faced. It is entirely possible, I think, that the radical atheism
of the times will turn out to be an early cop-out, an easy way
of avoiding the hard thinking and imagining that must be
done to rediscover a sense of the numinous and of the correspondence between man and the cosmos for our own stage of
human development. Most men, like Huxley's Savage, are
finally unwilling to settle for a de-deified humanity, believing, almost instinctively, that man's only future with promise
involves his maintaining a tension between himself and his
technology, or between himself and things. They will part
with their orthodoxies, and become heretical toward their
former religious conceptions about the nature and person of
God, before they will damn themselves to the bad logic of
those orthodoxies. They may say, like a character in one of
Hesse's novels, "I was satisfied too soon and offered myself to
Jehovah before I knew about Abraxas,"[36] or they may, reex-
amining Jehovah from new perspectives, find their earlier
god vehicle enough for new and greater experiences of the
transcendent. But either way they will discover that the wells
of theism, of the *mysterium tremendus et fascinans*, are
neither totally poisoned nor depleted. And when they dis-

35. Gardner, *Religion and Literature*, p. 100.
36. Pistorius, in Herman Hesse, *Demian*, trans. Michael Roloff and Michael
Lebeck (New York: Bantam Books, 1969), p. 93.

cover this, when they have formulated new means of conceiving of the transcendent—*of being able to experience it again*—then the almost incalculable guilt they have buried and repressed during these agnostic and boisterous years will burst out upon them, like some deep festering sore suddenly lanced, and demand to be assuaged in a calling of accounts. Then—we shall have our new Sophocles or our new Shakespeare. That is, we shall have him if we are lucky; for there have doubtless been critical eras in the history of man when the conditions for tragedy have been fulfilled except for the presence of the particular poet to compose it.

The form of tragic literature is still with us, despite the modern traditions of underground men and antiheroes which have threatened to undercut it. The plays of Beckett and the novels of Robbe-Grillet and Sarraute have perpetuated it in the very act of mocking it. Their authors have walked the tightrope with their art, attempting to steer a middle course between the older dramatic forms on one hand and a formlessness so total and nihilistic on the other that one slip of the foot at the wrong moment would have cost them the game. The tightrope—what Father Lynch calls the possibility of failure—has been the real measure of their genius. In the same way that blasphemy depends on a prior religious stance for its constitution in an antithetical role, the antitragic depends on the tragic to keep it alive at all. And as religion has a way of coming back, swallowing up antireligion and making it part of its revised creed and holiness, so will the tragic return, swallowing the antitragic and actually using it to gain new heights.

I know it is not enough merely to say this. We need some earnest, some pledge that it can happen in our time, or, if not in ours, in some later time. Is it really possible, we find ourselves asking, to create a tragic literature in our time which would do for our time what *Oedipus* or *Lear* did in theirs?

Such a literature would have to arise out of the kind of anguish so special to this century—or at least the one that

seems so special to it. The protagonist would have to bear the
burden of his age. The resolution would have to be absolutely
credible in terms of the present secularist mentality—no re-
coups like the one at the end of the book of Job, no ascension
into heaven after the crucifixion—just a psychic cleansing, a
real catharsis, a renewal of the person occurring through
fresh recognition of the essential juxtaposition of finite man
and infinite mystery. What would have to be called to mind
is more than the historically conditioned and therefore limited framework of a particular religion or specific set of religious beliefs. What we should require is the *immemorially*
religious, the symbolic and mythological acts which have been
repeated again and again in particular religious language and
particular religious occasion, but which, because they are
somehow expressive of the psychological dimension of man's
inner and outer life, transcend the particular expressions at
the same time that they lend credence to them. This is what
we have in the great Greek tragedies and in Shakespeare—
they *transfer*, from age to age and culture to culture, because
there is something innately and fundamentally true about
them, something true in a universal sense, beyond the domain
of their special *milieux*.

If our present culture is more completely secularist than
most of us wish it were, so that there is a kind of cosmic sense
of insecurity abroad, an aura of disillusionment and pessimism, and a consequent moral lassitude (which expresses
itself far more dreadfully in rampant opportunism, misrepre-
sentations, and ruthless competitiveness than in such phenomena as public nudity, obscene language, and the use of pot),
at least part of the reason for it is the absence of truly great
tragic images capable of gathering up the fear and anguish
and resentment men smother in their breasts and discharging
it in moments of tragic recognition. Such moments are, as
they have always been, the true occasions of religious emotion
and insight. They are what bind the people together with
mystical bonds, and permit, even publicly, a sense of tran-

scendence in the populace. Mere religious rites, that is, rituals maintained and continually performed by cultic groups, tend to lose their deeper significance as people become habituated to them; they become part of the environment and stand as much in need of renewal as the environment itself. But the moment of insight arising out of totally secular conditions, out of the profane world, and coming as the climax to a set of purely credible and profane actions—that has impact, that has authority, that is capable of galvanizing the populace from within its own accepted structures of reality.

I think there may be one example—one very significant example—of this secularized tragedy in our time in the movie *The Pawnbroker*, produced by Rod Steiger and based on the novel by the late Edward Wallant. The protagonist is Sol Nazerman, a Jew who survived the Nazi deathcamps and is now a pawnmerchant in a little shop in Harlem. The intense suffering he knew in the war years—he lost his wife and children, and witnessed the rape of his wife by Nazi officers before her death—has left in its wake a terrible callousness, a profound apathy, which is patently a kind of defense in a man who wishes never to be wounded so deeply again. He walks without emotion in one of the world's most notorious ghettos, never more than half-conscious of the crimes and outrages against nature there which are as vicious as any he witnessed in Germany. A parade of broken, anguished people brings the daily pathos of Harlem into his shop—a pregnant girl trying to pawn an engagement ring with a fake diamond, a teen-age drug addict needing money for a fix, a father agonized at having to sell a pair of bronzed baby shoes after the baby has died or grown up—but the pawnbroker, adamantly unresponsive, completes his transactions with impeccable *sangfroid*. The audience knows, however, that he is a man capable of passion. Something is happening to him. There are fissures and irruptions occurring in his psyche; what he thought he had repressed forever is beginning to crash through and enter his conscious world. The novelist accomplishes this trick of information with italicized passages, the movie producer with fade-ins and flashbacks. The bitter scenes from Germany are beginning to merge with the raw scenes of Harlem. Nazerman blinks and shakes his head—he sees policemen and thinks for a moment they are S.S. men.

The climax of this melding process occurs one day when a group of hoodlums appears in the pawnshop to rob the old man. The pawnbroker's assistant, a Negro–Puerto Rican boy named Jesus Ortiz, had idolized him and become a son to him, but, failing to find acceptance in that role, has thrown in with the hoodlums. Unexpectedly, one of the boys draws a gun and is prepared to shoot the old man. Jesus, confronted with an immediate choice, hurls himself against the gun and is killed. The boys flee, leaving the startled pawnbroker cradling the head of the dying Jesus. The effect of it all is to open the sluices in the old man's life; suddenly all the pressures from the past break through, and his humanity returns in a torrent. The agonies of Harlem are identical with the agonies of Nazi Germany. All men walk in the valley of the shadow of death, all men suffer from the evil in the universe, all men need redemption, all men need love, all men need each other.

At this point Steiger, in the movie, takes the license of the creative spirit to move beyond the symbolism of the novel. In the novel, Jesus is almost too obvious a Christ image. His death does return the old man to the world of the living—to the obligations and commitments of that world. But ignoring that, or perhaps transcending it, Steiger carries the business to yet another level. In the movie, the old man leaves the inert form of the boy on the sidewalk outside his shop, whither the boy has managed to crawl, leaves the sounds of the crowd that has gathered, including the hysterical accusations of the boy's mother that he has murdered her son, and staggers back inside the sanctuary of the shop. He stands for a few moments behind the desk of the broker's cage, clutching the top, his eyes blinded by tears. Finally his vision begins to clear, and we see, perhaps even before he sees it, what is there and what he is going to do. It is the slender, gleaming nail of a paperspike thrusting its way, piercing its way, into the world of our vision. Slowly, resolutely, as though there were nothing more natural or more necessary in the world, as though it were the most inevitable act in these or any similar circumstances, the old man poises his hand over the spike, then forces it down—down—down, until he has completely impaled himself. Then, clutching the bleeding hand, he closes the shop and goes away to rejoin the world of his relatives and acquaintances, and to begin there the necessary task of becoming involved once more in the lifestream of humanity.

Perhaps it is a gratuitous act, a totally useless act, from a pragmatic point of view. But from the point of view of man's psychological needs and compulsions, it is an unavoidable act, and a satisfying one. Here, just as the line of action is about to cross the precipice and fall off into resolution, the artist holds on a few seconds longer, bears it out a little further. He appropriates to the story he is telling this unspeakably sacred gesture from the wounding of Christ, the piercing of the hands. But it is more than a Christian gesture. There is something immemorial about the wounding, something universal, with reverberations in all the ancient mythologies. The protagonist clearly recognizes his guilt, and sees that he cannot any longer remain aloof from the mainstream of human activity and suffering. In accepting the wounding, he accepts life again. The wounding itself is an exchange, a wounding *pars pro toto*, that will save him from violent and total death. Save him? Preserve him to a world of agony and evil, where he will work out his redemption in sharing the burden of all humanity. This is the blinding of Oedipus or Gloucester, the madness of Lear, the exile of Dmitri Karamazov.

I know of no contemporary work of art which bears quite the same relationship to ancient tragedy that this movie does. The movie has, after all, become the essential theater of our technological era. And whenever I have seen the film I have observed the same effect upon the audiences: they leave deeply moved but dry-eyed. It is not a case like *Death of a Salesman*, which Miller hoped was a tragedy. Tragic situations cause men to weep; but tragic resolutions carry them beyond tears. The impact of the pathos remains; but something else, like a rainbow after the flood, also remains. The horror has done its worst, but has not vanquished the human spirit. It has cleansed the spirit—humiliated it, chastened it, purified it—but it has not destroyed it. And there is, for that cleansed spirit, a sense of presence in the world holding off the evil so it cannot accomplish its ultimate destruction. There is, whatever you wish to call it by, a renewal of the sense of the holy. Life, for all its terrors and angularities, is not entirely the hopeless mess it had appeared to be. Something has, to use Professor Krieger's word, *absorbed* the evil.

Many people who have just seen *The Pawnbroker* do not wish to talk about it immediately afterward. What they have been through, the agony and the ecstasy, is a religious experience, with levels so deep in their beings as to render them almost totally nonverbal. It is something rapturous, in which the soul beholds, precisely *through* the veil of suffering and temporality, the shape of something ultimate, eternal, and transcendent. And, unless we are willing to surrender beyond recovery the image of man as we have known him in the long traditions of Western thought—how many millennia would be required to expunge that image from the collective unconscious?—unless we are ready to bow to the darkness, and accept the chaos of a totally ahistorical future, that shape, that shapeless shape, that amorphous and inexplicable presence, is the most important aspect of our entire cultural picture.

Let me attempt a footnote. Huxley, it seems, has left us the problem in a kernel. God is necessary to explain the suffering of man. But if the suffering is alleviated the idea of God or his presence becomes superfluous. We have tended to take it for granted that the breakdown of Jewish-Christian thought in the centuries after the Renaissance has left us with very little feeling for the reality of God and, consequently, with a truncated, nontragical world. This is a warrantable assumption. But it is also possible, I think, that the same effect could have been rendered by a widespread, anonymous, and often unconscious attack on the reality of suffering. We have somehow established the implicit understanding in the modern world that suffering is never as bad as the mind makes it out to be and that therefore no individual has the right to complain to others of his misery. People doubtless suffer as much as ever before, but our reticence in dealing with personal anguish at a public level has robbed it of both its destiny and its transcendence. It deteriorates, just as the idea of God does, into illusion and confusion.

What *The Pawnbroker* achieves in singular fashion is the refurbishing of suffering as a universal, transcendent emotion, so that audiences are given some feeling again for the demonic in human affairs. God becomes a reality at the end of the film precisely because nothing else will answer the power of evil that has been caught in the story. Wallant and Steiger have overcome the docetism of evil and made it real. They have reified it sufficiently for Nazerman to crash up against it and accomplish purification. It is no longer so diffused, intangible, and unnameable as it has usually been in contemporary writings. The tragic vision is able to achieve tragic resolution. We have followed the curve of what Paul Ricoeur calls "the transition from the possibility of evil in man to its reality, from fallibility to fault,"[37] and are able to participate with the pawnbroker in accepting complicity and an ultimate release from the guilt of life.

The Savage is quite possibly right: we need to take anguish more seriously. As Jung and Fromm have been at pains to

37. Paul Ricoeur, *The Symbolism of Evil*, trans. Emerson Buchanan (Boston: Beacon Press, 1969), p. 3.

show us, no psychology takes it seriously enough that does not respect the significance of certain archetypal rituals in man's attempt to maintain sanity in his cosmos. The sense of universal guilt has not and will not be expunged in the space of a few generations—not when it has been bred into the human mind since the dawn of history and before. We are not yet prepared, as even the demiworld of Beckett and Robbe-Grillet attests, to give up the rite of repentance and expiation which is celebrated at the heart of formal tragedy. We need "something with tears," as the Savage says—and something to carry us beyond tears.

II.

Camus and After:

God in the Literature of Absurdity

Antonin Artaud, that revolutionist of the theatrical idea without whom the contemporary theatrical experience would be simply unthinkable, carried on, in the years 1923 and 1924, a most illuminating correspondence with the editor of *Nouvelle Revue Française*, Jacques Rivière. Artaud had submitted some poems which Rivière was unable to publish, but they interested Rivière so much that he invited the author to come to see him. What they said to each other on the occasions of that and successive visits we shall never know except through their letters, which preserve at least a fragment of their discussion. One matter, at least, had to do with Artaud's method of apprehending reality.

He wrote, "I suffer from a frightful disease of the mind. My thought abandons me at all stages. From the simple act of thinking to the external act of its materialization in words. Words, forms of phrases, inner directions of thinking, simple reactions of the mind—I am in constant pursuit of my intellectual being. Hence, whenever *I can seize upon a form*, however imperfect it may be, I hold it fast, lest I lose the entire thought."[1]

It is obvious, from Rivière's reply, that Artaud's poems had been rejected at least partly on the ground that they did not achieve coherent impressions. Rivière admitted that there were "awkward things and disconcerting oddities" in them,

1. "Correspondence with Jacques Rivière," trans. Bernard Frechtman, *Artaud Anthology*, ed. Jack Hirschman (San Francisco: City Light Books, 1965), p. 7.

but generously suggested that these might be due to "a certain quest" on the author's part and not to a lack of command over his thoughts. He was sure that Artaud could, with a little patience, eliminate divergent images from his works and manage the attainment of "perfectly coherent and harmonious poems."

When Artaud finally answered this letter, over six months later, he said that he had been annoyed by such a reply. He *knew* what was wrong with his poems; he had not wished an analysis of their faults; he could make them absolutely perfect if he wished; what he wanted, what he was really after from Rivière, was a confirmation that Rivière had actually beheld him for the rarity he was, "a mental case, an actual psychic anomaly." He did not care about the poems, he insisted; he *could* not care. He had wished only to exhibit to Rivière, who appeared to be extremely sensitive and perceptive, the phenomenon of a man who had undergone "a central collapse of the mind," whose very existence was being eroded by "something furtive which takes away from me the words which I have found, which diminishes my mental tension, which destroys in its substance the mass of my thinking as it evolves, which takes away from me even the memory of the devices by which one expresses oneself and which render with precision the most inseparable, most localized, most existing modulations of thought."[2] In a word, he had hoped to discover a friend as interested as he himself was in what he called "the subtlety, the fragility of the mind."

This time it was Rivière who delayed answering. Artaud wrote to chide him. When the reply came, Rivière said that he had delayed because he had had nothing to say. He was not disinterested, and had in fact been ruminating on the matter. "The fact that the mind exists by itself," he said, "that it has a tendency to live on its own substance, that it develops in the individual with a kind of egoism and without

2. Ibid., p. 11.

bothering to maintain him in harmony with the world seems, in our time, no longer open to question."[3] Paul Valéry's *Evening with M. Teste* was a brilliant example of the autonomy of the mind, of its self-propagation, its tendency to move out in all directions, oblivious of any responsibility to relate the whole man to the world before him. "There is a whole body of literature"—and here Rivière might be speaking of our own era as well as his—"which is the product of the immediate and, if I may say so, animal functioning of the mind. It resembles a vast field of ruins. The columns that remain standing in it are held up only by chance. Chance reigns there, as does a kind of dismal multitude. One might say that it is the most accurate and direct expression of the monster which every man carries within him, but which he actually seeks, instinctively, to fetter in the bonds of facts and experience."[4]

Had Artaud spoken of "the fragility of the mind"? "To put it more precisely," said Rivière, "this is how I see the matter: the mind is fragile in that it needs obstacles—adventitious obstacles. If it is alone, it loses its way, it destroys itself. . . . In order to grow taut, the mind needs a landmark, it needs to encounter the kindly opacity of experience. The only remedy for madness is the innocence of facts."[5]

The succeeding correspondence became increasingly intimate in its disclosures. Rivière's relationship to the brilliant but erratic writer became more and more that of a counselor, a confessor, an analyst seeking to help a man who felt himself sinking almost irretrievably into his own wild way of experiencing the world. To cries of self-doubt and lack of lucidity, the stable friend replied with assurance and confidence. A final effort to communicate with Artaud involved the editor in confession as well: he too had experienced the helplessness of which Artaud had spoken, and supposed it to be somewhat

3. Ibid., p. 15.
4. Ibid., pp. 15–16.
5. Ibid., p. 16.

normal among intelligent men. He had never doubted his
own reality, as Artaud had his; indeed, it seemed to hang over
him like a roof, somehow miraculously suspended and unable
to fall even when he saw no means of reaching it again.
Proust had spoken of "intermittences of the heart"; Rivière
preferred to speak of "intermittences of being," as though
personalities suffered from alternations in the intensity of
their existence or their ability to experience the world. He
felt certain that "a whole category of men are subject to shift-
ings of the level of being." "How often do we not suddenly
discover," he said, "when mechanically placing ourselves in
a familiar psychological attitude, that it has transcended us,
or rather that we have become surreptitiously unequal to it!
How often does our most habitual personage not appear to
us suddenly to be factitious and even fictive, owing to the
absence of the spiritual, or 'essential', resources that were
supposed to feed it!"[6]

"Where does our being go and from where does it return,"
he asked, "that being which all psychology until our time
pretended to regard as a constant? It is an almost insoluble
problem, unless one has recourse to a religious dogma, like
that of Grace, for example. I am amazed at the fact that our
age (I am thinking of Pirandello, of Proust, in whom it is
implicit) has dared raise it while leaving it in a state of a
question and limiting itself to anguish."[7]

There, in those remarkable letters, is a summary of what
has happened in modern literature as a whole. The phenomenon of "intermittences of being," or ontological palpitation,
has become the central fact, the controlling motif, in what
might conservatively be estimated as more than one-half the
important plays and novels of our time. The mind has played
its tricks and knocked over the boundaries; we are no longer

6. Ibid., p. 24.
7. Ibid.

certain of reality's shape or function. We live in a universe where nothing coheres, continues, or possesses constancy. There are times when, as Rivière indicated, it almost seems normal to stand outside the self and behold its pantomime as in a dream, to lose one's hold on reality and doubt if he will ever get it back again, to become disoriented, like a diver in deep waters, and not know where the surface is anymore. Some men, like Rivière, remain convinced of a penumbra of reality, of something lasting and certain even when the mind is subject to moods of evanescence and free-floating; others, like Artaud, abandon themselves almost thoroughly to the alternate movements of dissolution and coagulation, never quite sure, when things have dissolved beneath them, that they will ever coalesce again.

Ionesco has quite freely admitted that this sudden alternation from a solid to a less definable state was responsible for his play *The Killer*, that remarkable episode in which Bérenger discovers that the wonderful City of Light, which is the *ne plus ultra* of urban planning and development, is menaced by a ruthless killer. In the end, Bérenger is himself confronted by the killer. He is not frightened, however, because the killer is a small, impotent looking person. He tries to adduce arguments to "convert" the killer, to persuade him that what he is doing is wrong, that men deserve to live and not die; but the killer only answers each of his arguments with a sinister laugh. Gradually, in a horrifying process of attrition, Bérenger exhausts his arguments and realizes that the killer is right, men do deserve to die. He is no longer superior to the killer; he surrenders to his own death. And the chilling thing about the whole performance is that we realize that the killer does not truly exist, that he is the product of Bérenger's own imagination.

"The reality of the unreal, the unreality of the real."[8] Ionesco has said on numerous occasions that he is subject to

8. Eugène Ionesco, *Journal en miettes* (Paris: Mercure de France, 1967), p. 27.

unexpected mutations in temperament, to feelings of evap-
oration in which what is normally taken to be solid and
trustworthy in existence melts away and is no longer sound
or meaningful. The inspiration for *The Killer*, he says,[9] occurred on a warm day in June, toward noon, when he was
strolling through a country village. He was experiencing an
unusual feeling of tranquillity; even the barking of the dogs
as he passed seemed to harmonize and become melodious in
his mind. The sound of children's voices floated to him over
a sea of idleness. It was a perfect day, more perfect, he
thought, than those of ancient times, before the long history
of wars and modern brutalities. He walked and walked, without fatigue. Then suddenly, without warning, his impression
changed. The world became itself again. The joy was gone.
Everything was flat, stale, plain, dirty. And he enfleshed this
mercurial alteration in a play, where other men meet their
own impressions of a similar experience, and recognize them.

Camus, whose official training was in philosophy though
his predilection was toward the journalistic pulpit, attempted
to give official recognition to this phenomenon as a basis for
true philosophy—that is, a philosophy wrenched away from
the rationalistic direction it had been given by European
thinkers from Descartes to Hegel, and brought back into line
a plainer, less grandiose "philosophy of life" for the man in
the street. He was impatient with the rationalistic escape from
the world of hard facts, where men must live among objects
whose being is somehow different from their own, and where
they therefore have the feeling of alienation, of being strang-
ers in an absurd kind of universe. The first and most essential
question of philosophy, he said, is suicide—deciding whether
life is or is not worth living under the conditions, the only
conditions, by which it may be had; for absurdity is universal; it can strike any man in the face as he turns the next
corner on the street where he is walking; he can suddenly feel

9. Claude Bonnefoy, ed., *Entretiens avec Eugène Ionesco* (Paris: Éditions
Pierre Belfond, 1966), pp. 36–37.

the same slump, the same intermittence of being, that Ionesco felt walking through that country village.

The instinctive reaction of any man when he encounters the absurd is to try immediately to transcend it. He shakes his head, reorients his mind, says it must be something he ate or a change in the atmospheric pressure, and reaches once more for the penumbra, for Rivière's miraculously suspended roof overhead. If the feeling persists, so that it begins to occupy a kind of metaphysical centrality in the person's life, he is liable, like Kierkegaard, to attribute it to his human finitude and flee for certainty to the idea of God, who still holds all things together, even though they may appear, at the level of human experience, to cascade into the abyss.

But Camus was unhappy with Kierkegaard's resolution of this matter; it was just as much a dodge, he felt, as the rationalistic philosophies themselves. Kierkegaard wanted to be cured; he must not want that; he must be willing to live with his anxieties; he must not take the "leap of faith"; he must learn to coexist with the angularities of a world whose being he could not penetrate; somehow, the essence of being human, that which is peculiar to men as to no other creatures, is to be aware of a fundamental difference between the human psyche and all other orders of existence, and yet to choose to live among those other orders, to embrace the absurdity. Living, said Camus, is keeping the absurdity alive.

Camus was not original in this notion, of course. It had been coming to a head for some time in Western thought and literature. The phenomenon of the Underground Man, from Dostoevsky's *Letters from Underground* to Melville's *Bartleby the Scrivener* to Kafka's stories and novels, and leading to more recent manifestations such as the characters of Samuel Beckett or Ralph Ellison's *Invisible Man*, had already established a tradition of no-saying, of refusal to predicate human existence upon a too-easy acceptance of traditional philosophical and ethical schematizations, so that man blended harmoniously into the structure and movement of the universe. The beginnings were already there for an appreciation of absurdity, and for a mammoth repudiation of the old viewpoint that man is really in charge of the world he inhabits. Camus only figured as a receptor or transcriber, as the one qualified by the accidents of time and place and training to issue some important statements about man's experience of the absurd. The temperature was right; what had been hardening for a long time suddenly crystallized. It was there for everybody to see.

Since Camus, we have lived with a more or less radical awareness of the absurd.

The effect of this discovery led, in the world of art, to an emphasis on the principles of discontinuity and fragmentation. The Dadaists, and later the Surrealists, sensed the importance of this as the basis for a whole new approach to human expression. The world of representational art had long been imploded—that is, it had been done and redone in every period style until there was something almost unreal or untrue about it. It was like the effect of staring at any object too long: it begins to look unlike itself, to be a misrepresentation, to be grossly out of place. But what if the harmony and symmetry of existence were only a coverup for something else? What if, behind traditional ways of looking at the world, the world were really very different from the way it had been conceived? What if it appeared, in fact, to be chaotic and unordered, or at least to have an order of its own, still undiscovered by man, an order of another order, so to speak? Enthused by this new way of seeing, the Dadaists and Surrealists began to create an art which looked like antiart, in that it denied traditional artistic principles and techniques, but which has become increasingly accepted as a bonafide way of symbolizing reality. Hugo Ball composed phonemic poems, using only nonsensical words or syllables, and recited them to music. Marcel Duchamp retrieved for art the realm of the artifact and the commonplace by hanging a sign "Fountain"

on a public urinal. Robert Desnos and André Breton
labored over nonsyntactical aphorisms, and Desnos was
praised for his automatic writing, which he appeared to produce in a somnolent state. Apollinaire wrote a play in which
a woman became a man, and in which there was a talking
newspaper kiosk, initiating the revolt of inanimate objects
which was to come to climactic statement thirty years later in
Ionesco's plays *The Chairs* and *The New Tenant*. To many
persons, these hijinks were insupportable as art, and signaled
an era of decadence unlike any that had been seen since the
decay of the Roman Empire. But hijinks or not, it is our
judgment today, apart from any qualifications or disqualifi-
cations we would put upon them as art, that they are symp-
tomatic of a general disintegration of man's earlier, more
cohesive view of reality and of the dawning of a new, radically pluralistic and dissociated approach to truth and human
existence. We have all become increasingly aware of the dimensions of absurdity in our lives. Even if we are not prepared, like Artaud, to abandon ourselves voluntarily to the
surrealistic approach, we are more and more inclined, like
Rivière, to accept as normal those vacillations of the spirit, of
the levels of being, which in turn oblige us to be ever more
dubious of any kind of definitive or demonstrable reality.

One interesting effect is achieved by "radicalizing" the
surrealistic vision—that is, by accepting some insight, skimmed
perhaps from a dream or caught obliquely, out of the corner
of the mind's eye, inflating it until it fills out all the area of
one's consciousness, and then living in it, setting characters
in motion in it, as though it were the whole of reality, the
world we were all born to. Kafka did this to some extent.
Gregor Samsa, in *Metamorphosis*, did not merely *dream* that
he had become an insect; his horror was not a nightmare
bracketed between a sleeping and a waking; on the contrary,
he *did* become an insect; the alienation he experienced was
actually concretized in an irrevocable transmutation. Joseph
K., in *The Trial*, and K., in *The Castle*, did not merely imag-

ine that their world was distorted and troublesome; it *was* distorted and troublesome. There is some debate among the critics as to whether the distortion represented Kafka's own way of seeing the world or was an artistic device to call attention to a certain warpedness in human affairs. Günther Anders, for example, insists that Kafka employed the distortion in order to underline the kind of madness that so often passes as normal in the world. "By continuing to treat his madly distorted world as normal, Kafka conveys his sense of the even madder fact that madness itself is not recognized."[10] Regardless of one's position with regard to Kafka's intentionality, however, he must admit that the technique, of expanding the distorted glimpse into an entire world-view, has provided some of the most significant reflections on the human condition in our time.

Another writer, even more contemporary, who has capitalized on this ingenious technique is the English dramatist Harold Pinter. There is a certain quality about his plays— *The Room, The Dumb Waiter, The Collection, The Lovers, The Homecoming, The Birthday Party*—whose precise recognition eluded me for a long time. It was definitely there, in all of them, the same quality, but I could not quite define it. Then one morning I had one of those crazy little half-dreams we so often experience when we are almost but not quite awake. I don't remember the dream now, but I do recall that the progress of it, or the method of its procedure, caused me to give it some attention. The basis of the dream was not unreal at all; in fact, it was something actually derived from my conscious, workaday life. Only, because I was still in that rather free and easy state of semidreaming, that item from reality became a prism through which I saw the whole world. Everything, in other words, was distorted to give importance to that one true item. My professional life, my personal relationships, my work, my study, my menial tasks—*everything*—

10. Günther Anders, *Franz Kafka*, trans. A. Steer and A. K. Thorlby (London: Bowes and Bowes, 1960), p. 9.

was overshadowed by that one foolish little thing which had started the dream in the first place. Later, as I reflected on the typical way in which that half-conscious, half-unconscious process of distortion had occurred, it struck me of a sudden that it is exactly the technique that is common to all of Pinter's plays: they seize upon a single incident or frame of mind and then draw everything—an elongated action—through that perspective. *The Room*, for example, is an elongation of that fleeting, nameless fear that comes to all of us from time to time—a fear of nothing in particular, which causes us to shudder without quite knowing why, and then, like the shadow of a very small cloud, passes over and is gone. *The Lovers* is a sustained examination of another ephemeral mo-ment, the one in which a man or a woman wonders what it would be like if his or her mate were a passionate person stealing love on the sly under the nose of their humdrum alter egos. *The Homecoming* is a man's flashlike identifica-tion of his wife with the great whore-spirit of woman, drawn out into a full-length horror story. The action of any one of these plays could be halted in a moment by one's crying out that it is all unreal, that it is only a dream, only the grotesque expansion of something which, in its normal size, occupies but a small portion of reality. And yet, we begin to suspect that there is more "reality" to these matters than men once thought. What can they tell us about the id, about the mon-ster in the basement of our lives, about that whole subter-ranean area of our existence that undoubtedly influences our conscious thoughts and actions with enormous consequences? Perhaps Ionesco and Kafka and Pinter—and dozens of others who approximate the same technique of expanding the in-sight which has eluded the censors and slipped out of the unconscious—are valuable precisely to the extent that they refuse the plain meaning of the world we inhabit and deal in meanings occult and unusual.

You see, we are, as Shakespeare said, a problem to our-selves. We tend, or most of us do, to restrict our perceptual

range to certain comfortable levels. There is a point at which
the acquisitive, life-seeking instinct in us, what Freud called
the *Eros* instinct, reaches a peak and crests over into the with-
drawal, security-seeking syndrome, what Freud called the
Thanatos instinct. We assume that we know all we need to
know, that our data about the world around us are sufficient
to enable us to agree with more or less traditional concepts
of the meaning of life, and so we drive down our stakes there,
or even set them in concrete, on the principle that we shall
never again lengthen the lines or expand the essential area of
our domain. From that point on, life is primarily a matter of
reduction and contraction, of restatement and reenforcement,
of shoring up opinions and beliefs whenever and wherever
they show signs of sagging or collapsing. Not that we cease to
read and study and accumulate more information; on the
contrary, we have a high regard for sophistication, for the
process of refinement and embellishment within the borders
of what we have pontificated to be reality. There is a cycle by
which bourgeois cultures become genteel cultures, so Louis-
seizième, in fact, that there is nothing left to do but have a
revolution and become bourgeois all over again. This is what
is known as "implosion," filling a given area with more and
more content until there hardly appears to be room for more.
But there is something about us, most of us, that fights shy of
the open places in our boundaries, and of the possibility of
being sucked out of what we now call reality into the threatening deep, the darksome void, with its unrecognizable
planetoids and shapeless currents.

The main advantage of a literature of absurdity, therefore,
is that it disengages us from our habitual impressions of reality and releases us to the experience of a kind of ontological
formlessness and bewilderment in which we have the chance
to learn again. It blasts us out of our ghettos of imploded
knowledge and sends us often enough reeling through terri-
tories of being yet unmapped, undomesticated, and unfalsi-
fied. The opposite of implosion occurs: explosion. Suddenly

the mind, the psyche, the totality of the person, has its layers of protection and definition ripped away, and is exposed to the chilling winds and frightening noises of new space. It can be a breath-taking experience.

This was Artaud's idea of what the theater ought to be. He had an essential grasp of the metaphysical nature of theatrical origins—of the play as ritual, as enactment of sympathetic magic, by which mortals transcended themselves and entered into the fathomless mysteries and motions of the elements and the deities whose beings were not always distinguishable from the elements. The history of polite theater, he declared, was a mockery of such holy origins. Playwrights had inoculated drama, had made it safe for consumption. Seeing a play was like looking down the big end of a telescope: all one saw was a miniature version of ordinary life, encapsulated, controlled, and held at a safe distance. What *should* happen in the theater is just the opposite. The *other side* of reality ought to be brought into sight. Monsters should be let loose. Fantasies should sail through the air. Noises should become unbearable. And, through it all, the audience should be forced to look through the telescope *the other way*, so that what was distant is brought inescapably near, so that the soul is driven into madness and delirium.

What Artaud proposed, what he saw as the only alternative to the maddening processes of civilization and implosion, was to put the spectator at the theater in communication again with what he called "pure forces." He wanted a theater in which "violent physical images" would "crush and hypnotize the spectator," so that the spectator would be "seized by the theater as by a whirlwind of higher forces."[11] He spoke of "bringing metaphysical ideas directly onto the stage," and of "creating what you might call temptations, indraughts of air around these ideas."[12]

11. Antonin Artaud, *The Theater and Its Double*, trans. Mary C. Richards (New York: Grove Press, 1958), pp. 82–83.
12. Ibid., p. 90.

To the traditionalists among us, who are as conservative in matters of theater as in matters of religion and philosophy of life, this surely sounds like an invitation to the return of primeval and quintessential chaos. Nothing could sound more like the end of the world—and, indeed, there is something about the reports from Off-off-Broadway and experimental theatrical projects like the Living Theatre which inclines us to think that that is what the portents are pointing to today.

But, for Artaud, the very opposite was apparent: "In the anguished, catastrophic period we live in," he said, "we feel an urgent need for a theater which events do not exceed, whose resonance is deep within us, dominating the instability of the times."[13] What he conceived of, in the process of overthrowing our hallowed notions about time, space, and reality, was the possibility of our recovering once more that most vital apprehension of the deeper mysteries of our being, of the riddle of what Rivière, in their correspondence, had called the religious dogma of grace.

Is it possible, we are forced to ask ourselves, that our very religiousness has betrayed us into such infinitesimally small patterns of dogma and belief, into such routine ways of conceiving God and ourselves and the universe, that we have ended instead in blasphemy, muttering shibboleths and clutching idolatries while the world and larger truth spin away from us on their metaphysical errands? Could Artaud and the absurdists indeed be right, that we have defined our systems too minutely, so that, like Oedipus, saying *oida*, "I know," we know not, and are inwardly blind to the trackless immensities of mystery and the mind's possibilities there? Is the world of man's being really vaster and more intricate than we normally think of its being? Have we settled for habitual ways of seeing and feeling and knowing, so that we have essentially foreclosed the options originally open to human nature and human destiny?

13. Ibid., p. 84.

Artaud and the other Surrealists thought that we have, and they envisioned what they were doing—their experimentation, their interest in dreams and the unconscious, their nostalgia for childhood's innocence and openness, their acceptance of psychic phenomena—as an attempt to revitalize man spiritually, to open for him again the possibility of a *sur*reality, a reality transcending all the small and limited realities he tends to fashion in his ignorance or desire for security. Only in this *sur*reality, they felt, can we get beyond the "instability of the times," or the instability of *any* times, for that matter, and discover both the true infinity of God and the as yet unlimited possibilities of man.

Pinter's method of elongating an insight gained obliquely through the semiconscious mind, belonging not quite to the world of waking realities and neither entirely any longer to the unconscious, may thus be viewed as one avenue into a larger kind of reality. Seizing an unguarded moment in the psyche's ruminating, it holds it fast and forces it open more widely, so that it becomes a negotiable aperture into the whole shadowy realm of subliminal motivations and ways of feeling. The foray into the depths below the line of consciousness is of course neither definitive nor pure; that were entirely impossible, as the ego must always in a manner of speaking infect the id with its own presence and structures in order to recover anything from those nether regions for its examination and reflection. But the mind is expanded in the process, nevertheless; the ego becomes acutely aware of the existence of the id as a large, brooding, alter-universe, and is consequently humbled and intrigued. And it is entirely possible that that humility and intrigue is intimately related to the kind of humility and intrigue in ancient drama which is finally salvific and redemptive of human nature.

The sense of ontological horror evoked by Pinter's drama prompts us to ask, To what extent do our minds instinctively associate evil and the demonic with the id, with the human

unconscious and its basically sexual orientations, with the
dark and often tangled wilderness where the ego has always
been unable to imprint its shallow structures and intellectual-
izations? The answer is probably obvious. Our zeal for cate-
gorization, for building fences and thinking we have corralled
life's great intangibles, life's ambiguities, extends to evil in
much the same way that it extends to God and to goodness.
With a neoclassical desire for order, we have put each in its
proper place, and have assumed once more, with Protagoras
and Alexander Pope, that man is indeed the measure of
everything.

Again, however, the absurdists remind us that reality is
much more, and often quite *other*, than we had assumed it
to be. We have lived only on the surface, the thin frozen
surface, of aboriginal lakes whose depths are murky and unknown, and this is a time of melting. What monsters inter-
twine with angels, what indecipherable hulks with God and
light and orderliness? Joseph K., in Kafka's *The Trial*, thinks
he is innocent, and cannot understand why the warders have
come from the court to arrest him. Like Oedipus, he is so
righteous that he is indignant: he will search this matter out,
he will see that things are corrected, he will acquit himself,
and maybe all mankind in the doing of it. But in the end we
are quite sure that the whole accusation of guilt, the massive
indictment against his innocence, even the warders themselves, who finally carry K. to his death by an abandoned
quarry, have all materialized out of the vapors of K.'s unconscious mind, like Golyadkin in Dostoevsky's *The Double*
emerging out of the swamps of St. Petersburg. K.'s sin, his
crime, is not against some minor court or institutional law:
it is against nature itself, for conceiving it too neat and small.
K. is a bank clerk, a man accustomed to keeping things in
order. And that is his problem. That is the problem with all
of us. Reality—good, evil, righteousness, guilt—reality transcends our brittle notions of order. "Reason is a bitch," as
Luther said. We have drawn things too small. The conse-

quent madness of our times is in having to stand by while things are corrected, while the depths roil upwards and break through the surface, tearing, breaking, eroding, destroying the order we had imposed on it. Do we wonder why Ionesco's *Exit the King* is suddenly so classical in its dramatic concentration, its obvious restraint, in the midst of plays like *The Future Is in Eggs*, *The Motor Show*, and *A Stroll in the Air*? Its movement is like an equilateral triangle, proceeding from the hypotenuse deliberately to the opposite vortex, and then, when the vortex is reached, and the kingdom has shrunk until nothing but the king himself is left, the vortex opens wide, like a mouth, and sucks the king too into oblivion, leaving nothing at all on the stage but an eerie gray light where the throne had been. The play is an interlude of pessimism. It is a statement of what happens to man in a time when the depths break loose and the immemorial sources of being enter a season of agitation like storms under the sea. His kingdom, his civilization, possesses such recent and shallow roots into those depths that it simply cascades into nothingness.

Much of the so-called literature of the absurd may be used as an attempt to reinvest man with a proper sense of ambiguity in the world, especially moral ambiguity. What is evil, and is anything really free from it? What is good, and is anything really perfect in it? Ionesco's *The Lesson* strips down the professor who is giving instruction to one of his pupils, and reveals the manner in which knowledge is used for power and advantage, especially for sexual conquest; and the professor ends by killing the student, which may always be the finale to the transmission-of-learning process. In *The Killer*, to which allusion has already been made, Bérenger at last stands helpless before the cackling little fiend who has menaced the City of Light. Earlier, he possessed obvious superiority to the diminutive killer. But gradually, as he argued for the importance of human civilization on the grounds of its goodness and beauty and necessity, he realized how interlaced with selfishness and ugliness and pride these qualities really are in the human species, and therefore how specious his arguments. As in the execution of Kafka's Joseph K., we are left with the distinct impression that the protagonist really committed suicide because he was unable to face the tides of ambiguity and uncertainty erupting in his conscious existence.

Other writers are less despondent about the prospects of the return of ambiguity. There is a frolicksome air about Fernando Arrabal's *The Car Cemetery* and *The Condemned Man's Bicycle* and *The Architect and the Emperor of Assyria*, in which traditional patterns of morality or moral understanding are jumbled and distorted, but with childishness and naïveté generally seeming to triumph over all, even when they are the occasions for brutality and death to certain characters. John Barth's novels, especially *The Sotweed Factor* and *Giles Goat-Boy*, derive much of their enormous humor from the incongruities and irreverences arising out of the cultural shift of the times and the crush in which history, morality, and religion have inevitably been caught. The picaresque humor of both Joseph Heller's *Catch-22* and Ken Kesey's *One Flew Over the Cuckoo's Nest* likewise proceed out of the demise of certain cultural and spiritual values, and each in its way rescues something for survival out of the tumble and stench of decadent ideals. *Catch-22* goes all the way, a giant step beyond Hemingway's *A Farewell to Arms*, in which the protagonist defined a new individualistic morality by making his "separate peace," by depicting the protagonist who makes such a decision not as a serious hero, with a strict morality of his own, but as an absurdly comic figure whose only scruples plainly have to do with his own self-preservation. And Kesey's novel presents an obvious Christ figure who, at the opposite pole from a figure like Mauriac's Xavier Dartilongue or Bernanos's country prelate, is a scandalous, malingering, hard-drinking, drug-taking, loud-mouthed inmate in a mental institution. But in each instance there is something about the protagonist which we instinctively approve. Traditional structures of righteousness are obliterated;

we are in the presence of a chaos of values. Yet we rejoice in something ineradicably, inviolably human about them, something that perdures even when the traditions are in a shambles around them; nay, something that perdures, that evinces itself, *because* the traditions are in a shambles.

One novelist-dramatist who has gone all out to confuse the roles of good and evil, and thus confound the reader-viewer with a real sense of the world's ambiguity, is Jean Genet, who began writing as a prison inmate glorifying the world of the sodomist, the rapist, the thief, and the murderer. Curiously, more than one of the prisons in which Genet spent a part of his life were actually ancient monasteries, converted to darker usages in more recent years. Genet quite naturally therefore had a sense of the numinous or the holy as he contemplated life there, and saw the world of the prison, the hierarchy of prison life, in terms of saintliness and the orders of holiness. "We were carrying on the tradition of the monks," he wrote in *Miracle of the Rose*. "We belonged to the Middle Ages."[14] Manifestations of criminality, to this radically polarized way of thinking, became acts of devotion, with the gravity of ritual imparted to them: they were done for God, or, if not for him, for a "sickening impression of mystery" induced by memories of the Roman liturgy.[15] Genet's dramas, therefore, became highly secular facades, drawn from the world of pimps, prostitutes, and murderers, for rites and rhythms that are immemorially religious and that still carry with them, regardless of the offensiveness of the facade, a kind of primitive connection to the holy and transcendent. Even though what was considered sacrosanct and reverent in the long traditions of Western man is drawn down and defiled by association with the most repugnant kind of underworld or subworld imaginable, the opposite also occurs: association of that subworld with the supraworld of the holy and the righteous

14. Jean Genet, *Miracle of the Rose*, trans. Bernard Frechtman (New York: Grove Press, 1966), p. 9.
15. Cf. Jean Genet, *The Thief's Journal*, trans. Bernard Frechtman (Evanston: Greenleaf Publishing Co., 1965), pp. 29–30, 91–92, 184–85.

invests the subworld with a sort of holiness or sacrality. Categories are defied, shattered, abrogated. There is nothing, there is nowhere, not invested simultaneously by God and by evil. Man annuls this absurdity, or is redeemed in the midst of it, by worshiping God through evil. Thus, for Genet, the external dualities of existence are stitched together, held so that neither of them becomes a falsehood by eluding the other. Most people, especially the moral bourgeoisie, felt this scabrous dramatist, render life untrue by ignoring the dimension of evil; the God they think they worship is only a pale shadow of their own complacency and smugness, created out of their bankrupt spirits to rubber-stamp their patently thin and one-sided moralities.

Genet is not alone in regarding the God of most religious persons as the fictive product of their own self-deceiving desires for righteousness and security. Arrabal, whose distaste and utter hatred for the hypocrisies of Spanish Catholicism have led him to make some of the most vituperative comments on the church and its deity ever penned, had no qualms, in *The Architect and the Emperor of Assyria,* at having one of the characters assume the stance of a tenor in an opera and sing loudly, "Defecation on God! Defecation on his divine image! Defecation on his omnipresence!" N. F. Simpson, the English playwright, lampoons the triviality and ineffectiveness of most Christian prayers in a parody heard on a religious broadcast from the radio:

Prayer: Let us sing because round things roll;
Response: And rejoice that it might have been otherwise.
Prayer: Let us give praise for woodlice and for buildings
                sixty-nine feet three inches high;
Response: For Adam Smith's *Wealth of Nations* published in
                1776;
Prayer: For the fifth key from the left on the lower manual
                of the organ of the Church of the Ascension in
                the Piazza Vittorio Emanuele II in the town of
                Castelfidardo in Italy;

Response: And for bats.
Prayer: Let us give praise for those who compile dictionar-
            ies in large, rambling buildings, for the suitably
            clad men and women on our commons and in
            our hotels, for all those who in the fullness of
            time will go out to meet whatever fate awaits
            them; for the tall, the ham-fisted, the pompous;
            and for all men everywhere and at all times.
Response: Amen.
Prayer: And now let us dwell upon drugs, for their effects
            enlighten us; upon judo and hypnosis, for their
            effects enlighten us; upon privation and upon
            loneliness, upon the heat of the sun and the
            silence of deserts; upon torture, upon interroga-
            tion, upon death—for their effects enlighten us.
Response: Give us light, that we may be enlightened.
Prayer: Give us light upon the nature of our knowing; for
            the illusions of the sane man are not the illusions
            of the lunatic, and the illusions of the flagellant
            are not the illusions of the alcoholic, and the
            illusions of the delirious are not the illusions of
            the lovesick, and the illusions of the genius are
            not the illusions of the common man.
Response: Give us light, that we may be enlightened.
Prayer: Give us light, that, sane, we may attain to a distor-
            tion more acceptable than the lunatic's and call
            it truth;
Response: That, sane, we may call it truth and know it to be
            false;
Prayer: That, sane, we may know ourselves, and by know-
            ing ourselves may know what it is we know.
Response: Amen.[16]

Samuel Beckett, in *Endgame*, makes Hamm, the irritable invalid who is in charge of a decrepit household, call the "family" to prayer, and, after a few moments of silence, interrupt
it himself with the expletive, "The bastard, he doesn't exist!"
Yahweh-God, the deity of the Hebraic-Christian tradition,

16. N. F. Simpson, *A Resounding Tinkle* (London: Faber & Faber, 1958),
pp. 86–88.

is too radically historicized, too enmeshed in doctrine and dogma, too obliged to the expectancies of a conditioned religious viewpoint, to satisfy men who have peered into the smoking abyss of ontological reality and lived to write about it. Their word to a credulous people, or perhaps to one growing daily less credulous and not quite sure how to respond to its own irreverence, is essentially the same as that of J. B. Phillips: "Your God is too small." Too small, too limited, too defined, too lacking in mystery and otherness and transcendence. It is not the idea of accommodation or incarnation they object to; certainly the finite mind must have its god with a local habitation and a name. It is the *exclusiveness* they cannot bear; the rigidity, the inflexibility, the blind and imperturbable dogmatism.

Beckett has caught the pathos of the human condition on this score in his best-known play, *Waiting for Godot*. Of course it is not about God; if he had intended for people to substitute the name for Godot, as he told one reporter, he would have called him God. Godot. Maybe he had in mind *godillot*, he says, the French word for boot, because there is a lot of trouble with boots in the play. Or Godeaux, the name of a French cyclist, another person has suggested. Or Pierrot or Charlot, the famous clown figures. Still, it is about God. Ten million people cannot be wrong about that, however the author denies it. You feel it in the play. You know the bleakness, the starkness, the loneliness, as of a universe from which everything holy and vertical has withdrawn, and you know it *has* to be about God, or, what is worse, about the absence of God.

And the counterpoint to this, the beautiful counterpoint, the ironic counterpoint, which gives the play its vast genius, is the way Beckett refers again and again to the Mass, to the *locus classicus* of the presence of God in Western Christian thought. Not openly, of course. Not with shouts and lights and pointers. But subtly. Quietly. Almost imperceptibly. One of the tramps apologizes to the other: the *apologia sacerdo-*

talis, or confession of the priests before the service begins. There is some arguing about the thieves who were crucified with Jesus, and what the gospels say: the reading of the lesson. Pozzo and Lucky come on thé stage: an epiphany? Pozzo smokes his pipe and comments on the sweetness of the tobacco: incense? Lucky delivers a senseless monologue: the sermon. He falls, and Estragon says "To hell with him!": *descensus ad inferos.* In the second act, just before Pozzo and Lucky reappear, Estragon cries, at the top of his voice, "God have pity on me!" and, a little later, Vladimir says, "Christ have mercy on us!": *kyrie eleison.*

Of course the point is that nothing happens; or, as one critic would have it, since there are two acts in the play, "Nothing happens—twice." If Godot has come the tramps don't know it. They are still as they were. Nothing is changed. "We are not saints," says Vladimir, "but we have kept our appointment." Indeed they have; and the disclaimer does not really differentiate them from other saints who wait at the altar for a theophany which, so far as they can tell, has never come.

These fragments of the Mass glitter like pieces of broken glass in the mosaic of the play. What they were broken off from is no longer recognizable from the evidence in the play itself; we could not see it if we did not start with the prior fact of the Mass as a pattern. It is like some antediluvian culture reflected aeons afterwards in a few scattered artifacts and fossils. Light years have elapsed since the Mass had all that much meaning; now it is only an inarticulate deposit in the unconscious, something to trouble the dreams of the characters.

Is the matter clear? The God of the Christian tradition is superannuated, brittle, finite, obsolete. His finitude is reflected in these bits and pieces. There is not enough fire, not enough depth of meaning, left in the tradition to baptize them again into a sensible unity, into something with the dynamic necessary to relieve the waiting characters. That God and his cultural entourage are dead, passé, and man currently exists in a time between the times, when old deities cannot save and new ones have not been announced, when, indeed, man begins even to doubt whether there is enough energy left in the cosmos to produce new ones. For that is part of the picture in Beckett: of humanity at the end of its tether, unable to birth new gods.

But the ritual goes on, even after the demise of gods. It goes on in Genet and in Arrabal and in a dozen lesser playwrights. It goes on in the death of Randle Patrick McMurphy, in Kesey's *One Flew Over the Cuckoo's Nest.* It goes on even in *Waiting for Godot,* whose stichomythic, run-on lines form a strange kind of litany, like a eulogy in a sacred vault. The reason it goes on is that life transcends its gods. The God of the Western Christian tradition is part of the finite universe and has been relegated to that tradition and thereby dispensed with. The absurdists have moved beyond the tradition. They have witnessed its failure. But the dancing and the ritual never die. They go on forever, finding new and larger deities. They go on even when it hasn't appeared yet who the newer deities are. The impulse to celebrate is unquenchable, for it lies deep within the mystery of human nature itself. "Deep calleth unto deep" was the way the Hebrew writer put it. And, when the depths get choked with debris and sediment, so that the voice echoes only out of shallows unto shallows, then it is time for some new explosion to occur, for the bottom to be knocked out again, so that there is room for resonance once more.

This, whether the individual authors are conscious of it or not, is the major concern of absurd literature. Martin Esslin, who wrote the important document called *The Theatre of the Absurd* in 1961, revised it for republication in 1968, and one of the notable things about the new edition is a concluding chapter in which he says unequivocally that the writings of absurd dramatists, hallucinative and schizophrenic and ridiculous as they often are, represent a basic return "to the original, religious function of the theatre—the confrontation of man with the spheres of myth and religious reality."[17] "In expressing the tragic sense of loss at the disappearance of ultimate certainties," he says,

> the Theatre of the Absurd, by a strange paradox, is also a symptom of what probably comes nearest to being a genuine religious quest in our age: an effort, however timid and tentative, to sing, to laugh, to weep—and to growl—if not in praise of God (whose name, in Adamov's phrase, has for so long been degraded by usage that it has lost its meaning), at least in search of a dimension of the Ineffable; an effort to make man aware of the ultimate realities of his condition, to instil in him again the lost sense of cosmic wonder and primeval anguish, to shock him out of an existence that has become trite, mechanical, complacent, and deprived of the dignity that comes of awareness. For God is dead, above all, to the masses who live from day to day and have lost all contact with the basic facts—and mysteries—of the human condition with which, in former times, they were kept in touch through the living ritual of their religion, which made them parts of a real community and not just atoms in an atomized society.[18]

What the experience of absurdity does, in other words, is to open us to illimitable new possibilities for both God and mankind. New possibilities threaten the hell out of us, to be sure. There is nothing more disconcerting or nightmarish than to wake up, like a character in Kafka, and find that all the old signposts have been moved about and that even the whole landscape, which in this case could be called a soulscape, has been put in disarray. And yet there is definitely a point at which deliberate immersion in the experience of absurdity becomes necessary because the facts themselves, the hard, tangible, historical facts of our existence, have become facetious and absurd. Their very finiteness betrays us. We had trusted them so heartily, had relied on them so completely, that they were actually compelled to fail us. Else we

17. Martin Esslin, *The Theatre of the Absurd* (London: Penguin Books, 1968), p. 392.
18. Ibid., p. 390.

had ended in the idolatry of facts and things, and worshiped gods of our own composition.

It is interesting, and somewhat less ironic than it first appears, that the sense of the tragic, and therefore the possibility of authentic tragical theater, has actually become stronger during the period of absurd writings than it was for the two or three centuries before our own. Numerous playwrights, including Camus and Sartre and Anouilh, have exhibited an ineluctable fascination for classic texts of tragedy, and have continued to rework, in strange and compelling ways, the themes of Aeschylus and Sophocles and Euripides. What accounts for this? What indeed but the rediscovery, through modern arts and letters, of the thing Esslin called "the basic facts—and mysteries—of the human condition," of that lost "dimension of the Ineffable," which alone is capable of expanding the mind's horizons and inducing in man the kind of ultimate and redemptive humility that classical drama is all about.

There was an element of absurdity, we are certain, in the great tragedies themselves. You *sense* it in a play like *Orestes* or *The Bacchae*. Chairs and other furniture did not overwhelm the protagonists, as in a play by Ionesco, or boots and hats, as in a work of Beckett; the paraphernalia of existence had not risen in revolt and added a dimension of ridiculousness to the way men perceived reality. Yet the dialectic between the protagonist and the world around him was acutely drawn and starkly experienced: the *isolato*, as depicted today by Kafka or Heller or Ionesco, has its artistic and metaphysical roots at least as far back as ancient Greece.

No one felt more strongly than Artaud the debacle, the almost total absence, of tragic theater in the early years of this century. Everything had become domesticated and eviscerated, he said. Men no longer came to the theater for a religious confrontation. All drama had become drama of manners. Playwrights showed nothing but thin and futile reflections of everyday existence. It was a vicious cycle: men grew sicker from seeing such theater, and theater grew sicker from reflecting such men.

"The contemporary theater is decadent," said Artaud, "because it has lost the feeling on the one hand for seriousness and on the other for laughter; because it has broken away from gravity, from effects that are immediate and painful—in a word, from Danger."[19]

Artaud understood what the ancients, who often followed their searing tragedies with uproarious comedies, understood, namely, that real comedy, comedy which, as Nathan Scott has said, "refuses the experiment of angelism" and will not let us forget that we are fashioned out of dust,[20] is possible only in a world formed essentially by the tragic viewpoint and therefore extremely sensitive to man's highly tenuous position in the universe. The theater of the boulevard, for all its wit and cleverness, had missed this truth entirely. Therefore, said Artaud, let us propel this comedy which is not comedy and this tragedy which is not tragedy into such extreme forms, such ridiculous forms, that the absurdity of it will become apparent, and the entire surface of life as men now know it will crack and become marked by great fissures, through which will waft the phantasms of a deeper and more serious consciousness, repelling some but drawing others into the mists and vapors until they have committed suicide of the mind and been born again into a new way of seeing and feeling.

The result, as we know, was a theater which is neither comic nor tragic, but both, and never more one or the other than when they are truly together. Our impulse, when things are most tragic, and the world is dissolving beneath our feet, is to laugh—perhaps the same hysterical laugh that Kafka was forever laughing at the wrong moments in life. And it is, on the other hand, when things are most ridiculous and the in-

19. Artaud, *The Theater and Its Double*, p. 42.
20. Nathan A. Scott, Jr., *The Broken Center* (New Haven: Yale University Press, 1966), p. 101.

congruities of our existence are most in evidence before our very eyes, to be scared out of our wits, to tremble and weep and blaspheme, for we see in the broken texture of the comical the darkness of the very primeval abyss, yawning like the maw of some great animal, waiting to devour us.

One of the great questions, probably on the underside of all our minds, is whether man can live from day to day in a more or less uninterrupted consciousness of the absurdity, the high tenuousness, of his condition, or must not, perforce, inure himself to the terrific pressures of such a vision. Can we continue to function as men under such a penumbra of dread and uncertainty? Must we not manage somehow to congeal new levels of immediate reality as we go along, living, as it were, from explosion to explosion, but with a manner of calm and fortuitousness in between?

There are no hard and fast answers, of course. Some persons undoubtedly have more capacity for suspension and irresolution than others, for living on the tightwire between solidification and chaos without irremediably losing their balance in either direction. Others, conditioned by temperament or bodily chemistries or other factors, crave the immediacy of certainties, the solid comfort of timetables and charts and hard data, the obdurate facts of a world not yet dissolved into its pluralistic components even though it is indubitably composed of them.

André Breton, the author of the Surrealist *Manifestoes*, expressed hope that men would continue to grow in their perception of new levels of reality, and that eventually they would discover how to live with *sur*reality, with a vision simultaneously aware of both disjunctiveness and continuity in the world. Who can say but that what he had in mind was only another, admittedly more secular, way of saying what Teilhard and the Whiteheadian theologians have been saying all along about growing into Christ, into the Christ who, while rooted in finitude through a birth and ministry and death, is nevertheless cosmic and ubiquitous, drawing all men to himself?

At any rate, whatever our propensities for keeping the absurd alive in our midst, for living with the *danger* Artaud spoke of, we know that the experience of the absurd does unsettle us from our too-small theologies and return us to the churning, smoking abyss, to what Paul Tillich called "the God beyond God," and the possibility that grace has grasped the world more completely, more utterly, and more irrevocably, than we had ever believed. It prevents that premature solidification, that idolatrous fastening upon penultimate things, which is the bane of all truly religious response to our condition, and which is responsible in every age for the indiscretions and distortions of the spiritual consciousness corrected or abandoned in the text. It reminds us ever and again of what it means to be men, to be persons, to be human beings, made to walk among sticks and stones and all things tangible, yet abutting on mysteries of mind and meaning too vast for any argosies that have yet put sail upon them. It, and it alone, finally makes possible our accepting our acceptance and, with any significant dimension of true reality, hearing what we have been pleased to call the gospel.

Camus's instinct thus appears to have been a sound one: we *shouldn't* follow Kierkegaard in making a leap, at least not any leap construed as being one that carries us out of or beyond the human condition; we should turn instead *into* the absurd, into the very essence of man's anguish, where the answer to the riddle of his nature must lie. And we learn, in the absurd, not just from Camus but from absurdity as a phenomenon in the whole world of letters, that God inhabits the absurd, and that there is therefore reason to laugh and rejoice and enjoy ourselves, even though we are in danger and fear for our very being. It is *his* world that is absurd to us, and it is only the vision of absurdity that prevents our disastrously appropriating it as *our* world and falling into the sin immemorial, of trying to be as God.

III.

Fulfillment as Carnal:

God in the Literature of Sensuality

Man exists in a world of things, and the matter of his relationship to them is perennially troublesome to him. What are his connections to corporeal reality? How do the materialities of his environment affect who he is? In what ways is he the victim of the "organic conspiracy," and in what sense, if any, does he transcend it? The questions are never really settled, for they recur endlessly. Their epigram may after all be that rather definitive statement in Sherwood Anderson's *Tar*, that "There is a lot to think about you never can really think about." That is, the human mind is so utterly involved in the relationship under dispute that it can never arrive at any completely satisfying answers; it must finally disqualify itself from rendering any judgment. As Merleau-Ponty has so convincingly demonstrated, even so-called empirical evidences are hopelessly warped by the perceiving instruments themselves, so that both sensation and judgment have lost what was once assumed to be their self-evident clarity. " 'Sense experience' has become once more a question for us."[1]

Obviously the question is anthropological, for it bears upon the nature of man and how he regards himself as being related to the universe. But it is also theological, for it raises in turn certain primal questions about ancient mythologies dealing with creation and man's relationship to the *Ur*-power or force which shaped things as they were in the beginning. Whenever and wherever the Hebraic account of first and last

1. M. Merleau-Ponty, *Phenomenology of Perception*, trans. Colin Smith (London: Routledge & Kegan Paul, 1962), p. 52.

79

things has been accepted without questioning, matter has not been problematic. But when and where dubiety has arisen, so has the problem. The paradigm in our own time is of course Sartre's Roquentin, in *Nausea*, for whom the cold, distantiating sense of vertigo rises like an inner tidal wave as he stares at the root of a chestnut tree and realizes what an infinite ontological chasm separates him from its pure *thingness*, its uncompromising *ensoitude*. Western man is today more radically conscious than he has ever been of the irreducible and unrecoverable particularities in his achievement. "Posited, from the start, as *not being man*," says Robbe-Grillet, "they remain constantly out of reach and are, ultimately, neither comprehended in a natural alliance nor recovered by suffering."[2] It is no wonder, therefore, that Norman O. Brown should declare that "Christ, the fulfillment, is not an abstract idea but a human body. All fulfillment is carnal, *carnaliter adimpleri*,"[3] or that Sam Keen, following Brown's lead, should announce the death by gnosticism of theology itself unless the ailing science is suddenly revived by massive injections of carnality. "Theology is, at best," he says, "phenomenology."[4] Long centuries of intellectualization and refinement have produced a religion which is, despite all its talk of blood and incarnation, quite bloodless and docetic, basically altered in its manner of honoring the world and disengaged from the soil which first nourished its dark myths. The question must be put again whether Augustine was not a better theologian for having been a great sensualist, and whether the same was not true, in varied ways, for such figures as Anselm and Luther and Kierkegaard and Tillich. We must reject almost peremptorily those simulated theologies which pretend to any tidiness, as though reality had been shrunk to the proportions of a theorem or a system, and turn

2. Alain Robbe-Grillet, *For a New Novel: Essays on Fiction*, trans. Richard Howard (New York: Grove Press, 1965), p. 70.
3. Norman O. Brown, *Love's Body* (New York: Vintage Books, 1966), p. 222.
4. Sam Keen, *To a Dancing God* (New York: Harper and Row, 1970), p. 157.

again to those humped-up earth faults whose orderless and intractable heaps defy method in its very teeth.

Conrad Bonifazi, in *A Theology of Things*, has provided some initial probings in the right direction.[5] He cites, for example, the experiments in sensual deprivation conducted by psychologists and empirical scientists. People quickly hallucinate when isolated from customary sensory stimuli. He notes also Ashley Montagu's research into the function of the skin. Mammals lick the skin of their newborn, says Montagu, not merely for cleansing but in order to stimulate the nerve-ends and initiate the operation of the urogenital and gastrointestinal tracts; if for some reason the licking does not take place the newborn do not survive, because their physiological systems remain unalerted to the need for functioning. Human beings undergo a similar cutaneous stimulation through the longer period of labor required for their passing through the birth canal. Persons who are delivered by Caesarean section, thus averting this passage, are frequently discovered in later periods of life to be suffering from bowel or bladder deficiencies. The route to achieving the biblical desideratum of "dominion over things," says Bonifazi, is not a direct one which circumvents such matters as these; it necessarily lies *through* the experience of things or the experience of sensory relationships. Man is not man apart from these relationships, and he is most fully himself only in proportion to the degree that he realizes their importance. In the words of D. H. Lawrence, "We don't exist unless we are deeply and sensually in touch with that which can be touched but not known."[6]

"Deeply and sensually in touch with that which can be touched but not known." That is a very simple truth—but also a very profound one. Man *needs* things. He cannot exist apart from them. They are more intimately related to him

5. Conrad Bonifazi, *A Theology of Things* (Philadelphia: J. B. Lippincott Co., 1967).
6. D. H. Lawrence, "Non-Existence," *Complete Poems*, vol. 3 (London: Heinemann, 1939), p. 41.

and his feelings than he is often able to suppose. Regardless of how insistently the spiritualists warn us away from them lest we idolize them, there is something about human nature that will not endure a separation from them, that returns to them in spite of caveats and threats and barriers. It is almost as if our very health or salvation depended upon them, upon rediscovering from time to time those vast diurnal rhythms linking us to seas and seasons, to chthonic beasts and ancient oaks, to pearls and pomegranates, to horses and moss and ferns, in short, to any of those "forms and images" which Wordsworth in *The Prelude* praised as having "a breath/ And everlasting motion" capable of restoring the human soul.

Emerson felt as much, and suggested that the fields and woods "minister" to man through some kind of "occult relation between man and the vegetable." He knew that such a relation is not verifiable and that "the power to produce this delight does not reside in nature, but in man, or in a harmony of both," and he recommended that the pleasures of the relationship be used with temperance. "For nature is not always tricked in holiday attire, but the same scene which yesterday breathed perfume and glittered as for the frolic of the nymphs, is overspread with melancholy to-day. Nature always wears the colors of the spirit. To a man laboring under calamity, the heat of his own fire hath sadness in it."[7] Despite this, however, Emerson believed that a sense of the salutary comfort of nature is one of the highest pleasures man can realize, and that its effect is "like that of a higher thought or a better emotion coming over me, when I deemed I was thinking justly or doing right."[8]

A similar motif runs throughout the writings of Hermann Hesse, the German novelist so popular in the American counterculture of recent years. An instance of it occurs in *Demian*,

7. Ralph Waldo Emerson, "Nature," *Representative Men, Nature, Addresses and Lectures* (New York: Houghton, Mifflin and Co., 1883), pp. 16–17.
8. Ibid.

in the scene where Emil Sinclair and the strange theologian-musician Pistorius lie staring into the fire on Pistorius' hearth. Recalling this moment later, Sinclair reflects:

> Even as a young boy I had been in the habit of gazing at bizarre natural phenomena, not so much observing them as surrendering to their magic, their confused, deep language. Long gnarled tree roots, colored veins in rocks, patches of oil floating on water, light-refracting flaws in glass—all these things had held great magic for me at one time: water and fire particularly, smoke, clouds, and dust, but most of all the swirling specks of color that swam before my eyes the minute I closed them.[9]

The "long gnarled tree roots" recall, or, more accurately, *anticipate*, Roquentin's experience of existential nausea in Sartre's story, though here there is no suggestion of anguish; on the contrary, Sinclair delights in immersing himself in the phenomenal world. He is fully aware that the "confused, deep language" he hears may be only an act of psychological ventriloquism on his part, and that the ambiguities of the relationship are rendered all the more insoluble by his own subjective involvement. He says:

> The surrender to Nature's irrational, strangely confused formations produces in us a feeling of inner harmony with the force responsible for these phenomena. We soon fall prey to the temptation of thinking of them as being our own moods, our own creations, and see the boundaries separating us from Nature begin to quiver and dissolve. We become acquainted with that state of mind in which we are unable to decide whether the images on our retina are the result of impressions coming from without or from within.[10]

That is of course the dilemma, that the line between objectivity and subjectivity becomes dissolved, so that, in the opin-

9. Hermann Hesse, *Demian*, trans. M. Roloff and M. Lebeck (New York: Bantam Books, 1968), p. 87.
10. Ibid., p. 88.

ion of a *chosiste* like Robbe-Grillet, nature is unwarrantably and unnecessarily humanized and tragedified. Yet Sinclair goes on to insist, much as Emerson did, that this is really evidence of the important link between man and the world around him, and of a kind of oversoul "whose essence we cannot know but which most often intimates itself to us as the power to love and create."[11]

Nor can we reflect on Lawrence's phrase about being "deeply and sensually in touch" without thinking of Camus, whose importance in modern letters, Thomas Hanna assures us, owes much to the fact that he was a "tough sensualist" who accepted the impersonality of the universe without surrendering his belief in the essential somatic relationship of man to his environment.[12] Meursault, in *The Stranger*, is a classical instance of man's aloneness or apartness in the world, of his basically "alien" nature; and yet it is almost impossible to imagine a character more sensually devoted to the world around him. His mother's coffin, the cup of coffee there, the weariness of the trip back, the languoressness of a sunny afternoon, the loveliness of a woman's body, the heat of sand dunes, the glint of light on whitecaps in the Mediterranean, the brick walls of a prison cell, the tinkle of an ice-cream vendor's bell outside, the fragility of an old newspaper clipping—these things are preternaturally real and close to him. His awareness of difference, of being a man or a stranger in a world composed of such things, only heightens his sensitivity to them. Or perhaps it is the other way around: his sensitivity to them makes him all the more aware of being a man. "When Camus looks at the 'pathetic' creature called man and at the 'indifference' of the natural world and says yes to these things, finding them beautiful," says Hanna, "he is not in the least a nature-loving Greek pagan."

11. Ibid.
12. Thomas Hanna, *Bodies in Revolt* (New York: Holt, Rinehart, and Winston, 1970), pp. 188–95.

The comparisons with the ancient past are, finally, pointless, inasmuch as the ancient past was a mythic past; and when the mythic consciousness saw the world as "beautiful" it was with totally different eyes which saw a totally different universe, whose very existence, causality and personality were categorically separate from the depersonalized universe of the modern conceptual consciousness. Camus, indeed, loved sun, women, water and a good fight, but he loved these things without the slightest illusion or sentimentality: they were exactly what they were amongst the shifting relativity of all things that are. Nothing could be absolutized, finalized or deified. There was no ultimate meaning to anything—to human life or the world.

What I am saying is that Camus had totally accepted the modern, depersonalized and relative universe without the least trace of rancor or disappointment. It is one thing for men of the twentieth century to prattle about a relativistic cosmos, but it has been a totally separate matter to be able to open oneself somatically in total behavioral acceptance of this. Camus could do this.[13]

There is truth in this, of course, though it should also be said that none of us, including Camus, is *totally* divorced from former opinions about man and the universe. When Camus wrote in "Retour à Tipasa," seven years after the war, of his journey back into the sun-and-seascape of Algeria and his rediscovery of "the old beauty, the young sky" whose memory had never deserted him and had in the end protected him against despair, he sounded very much like the Wordsworth of "Tintern Abbey" who said that

> Nature never did betray
> The heart that loved her; 'tis her privilege,
> Through all the years of this our life, to lead
> From joy to joy: for she can so inform
> The mind that is within us, so impress
> With quietness and beauty, and so feed
> With lofty thoughts, that neither evil tongues,
> Rash judgments, nor the sneers of selfish men,
> Nor greetings where no kindness is, nor all
> The dreary intercourse of daily life,

13. Ibid., pp. 192–93.

Shall e'er prevail against us, or disturb
Our cheerful faith, that all which we behold
Is full of blessings.

Near the end of his life, the Frenchman who had written so
eloquently and passionately of resistance and rebellion was
speaking of writing "a vast novel" which would possibly concern itself with "a certain kind of love."[14] He appears to have
come around to what Norman O. Brown calls "an erotic view
of life," a view undeniably present at least subliminally in
all of his writing and which finally won out in a tremendous
consciousness of the need for reunion. No ultimate work of
genius, he said in "Retour à Tipasa," has ever been founded
on hatred or contempt. "In some corner of his heart, at some
moment in his history, the real creator always ends by re-
conciling."[15] Camus had not, in other words, settled for an
infinitely discrete and unrelated universe where human consciousness is lived out pitilessly in the midst of obdurate and
incommunicative nature. His own "invincible summer," as
he once called it, continued to summon him back to the possibility of some mystical relationship, some fresh and hopeful
resolution of the ageless antinomy between soul and matter.
How he would have resolved it, had he lived, would now be
mere speculation; but the problem was by no means closed
for him. Perhaps there is instruction in something Hanna
notes about the visit he once made to Camus's little office in
the Gallimard publishing house in Paris. On one corner of
the piled-up desk lay several blackbound copies of Karl
Barth's theological works; on the opposite corner was a copy
of *Lady Chatterley's Lover*. "I keep things in balance," said
the man who had once written an M.A. thesis on Neoplato-
nism and Christianity.

Lawrence's influence on the whole subject of sensuality in

14. Cf. Germaine Brée, *Camus* (New York: Harcourt, Brace, 1964), p. 254.
15. *"L'Artiste en prison,"* Camus's preface to *La Ballade de la geôle de Reading* by Oscar Wilde, trans. Jacques Bour (Paris: Falaize, 1952). Cited by Brée,
Camus, p. 239.

modern letters is especially profound. In some ways it is impossible to go beyond him. Radicalizing the preoccupation with nature and bucolic virtues which he inherited from such nineteenth-century novelists as George Eliot, Olive Schreiner, and Thomas Hardy, and even more especially their concern for the deep and often fatal attraction between the sexes, he made inestimable contributions to the later work of such writers as Henry Miller, Vladimir Nabokov, Lawrence Durrell, Jack Kerouac, Allen Ginsberg, William Burroughs, and Richard Brautigan. Few writers, unfortunately, have had a worse press than Lawrence. He has been called everything from "pornographer" to "blasphemer" to "irrationalist."[16] Damaging as the first charges are among generally puritanical and conservative readers, the last has been particularly devastating in drawing room circles and academic society. This is so partially because of the reputation and influence of some of the critics who have freely brandished it, among them no less a figure than T. S. Eliot. F. R. Leavis was certainly right, it seems to me, in championing Lawrence against Eliot's denigrations that he was not only "sexually morbid" and lacking in "any moral or social sense" but was grossly nonintellectual to boot.

If Eliot himself had a major fault, it was surely that he was too much the rationalist, too much the product of Western *Aufklärung*. He caught the brittleness and hollowness of the modern situation precisely because he was so personally afflicted by those very qualities. Only when he turned to the medieval, to the themes of love and death and sacrifice, to religion, did he become liquid and lugubrious in his poetry. The mystery of these things attracted him as if by the opposite of his own nature, and, in *Murder in the Cathedral*, *Ash Wednesday*, and certain sections of *The Waste Land* and *The Four Quartets*, he reached his finest level in those moments

16. For a recent examination of these charges, see Horton Davies, "The God of Light and the Dark Deities," *Religion in Life* 38, no. 2 (Summer 1969): 229–41.

when the intellect drowned itself in the imagery of sex and the blood of communion. He felt by intuition the importance of the sensory in mythology and in medieval spirituality, but was apparently incapable of confronting his own world with anything like sensual immediacy. Lawrence appropriated the earth directly, without intervention of mind or dogma, and Eliot simply could not understand this; he inveighed against a man who appeared to write, as he perceived it, with neither intelligence nor appreciation for civilization. But the judgment of time is beginning to vindicate Lawrence and uphold the contention of Leavis that he exhibited a "transcendent intelligence" wholly inseparable from his particular creative genius. As Leavis said, "It is Lawrence's greatness that to appreciate him is to revise one's criteria of intelligence and one's notion of it. Eliot's finding him incapable of thinking is a failure of intelligence in himself."[17]

Many persons, especially those nourished in a Western intellectual tradition, have the same difficulty with Lawrence and with sensual art in general that Eliot had. We had been instilled with a dualism which teaches us to subdue the flesh, even to mortify it, if necessary, in order to exalt the spirit; and this dualism, originally appropriated from the East, has been further confused by introducing rationalism into the picture and identifying spirit with mind. The mind must maintain its superiority in order to maintain order, to fend off original chaos. We have pulled ourselves up by the bootstrap of thought, and, however wearisome it becomes, we must never let go the strap. "Blowing the mind," in a society like ours, becomes equivalent to a kind of moral capsizing; it means either destroying the foundations of that society, or, what may seem infinitely worse, exposing the fact that those foundations never really supported it anyway.

The contemporary churchman has a particular problem in all of this, for he has received a tradition in which God tends

17. F. R. Leavis, *D. H. Lawrence: Novelist* (New York: Clarion Books, 1969), p. 27.

to be equated with mind and order, with the abstract intelligence which keeps the seas in their boundaries and the categories of existence in their places. Religion, conceived on this master analogy, devolves into right-thinking, into knowing and doing, but especially knowing, into emulating the intelligence which stands as a sentinel against the evidences of change, flux, and movement. Doxologies cool and harden into dogmas, and the transports of one age become the tests of faith in another. Everything must be kept where it is, fixed and frozen, lest the world dissolve beneath us.

What most religious persons appear to want, says Arthur McGill, is a "divinely immobile" situation, a god of *stasis* who presides over an organized, finalized kind of existence where all chance has been removed:

> People want their world to be built out of indestructible particles. They want their knowledge to be grounded on solid facts. They want their security to be guaranteed by invincible weapons and impregnable defenses. Above all, they imagine their gods in this same way. Since to be real means to be heavy and static, to be supremely real is to be supremely heavy and supremely static. And so men worship a God who has eternal, immovable, self-contained absoluteness. Their God not only does not change or move, but by His own inner nature He cannot change or move. Mercurial activity can have no place in His existence; His divinity lies in His unlimited heaviness. And alongside of this immovable God stand all His immovable believers, whose lives show the same inflexible rigidity, and who cannot move or dance under the weight of their heavy "faith."[18]

In this kind of thinking, the great ages of passion and feeling must inevitably lie in the past; they belonged to times of formation; but now that patterns have emerged there is no place for them; they would threaten the patterns and disturb the divine equilibrium. Even the eschatologically-oriented sectarians are not really open to change: the "end" of all

18. Arthur McGill, *The Celebration of Flesh: Poetry in Christian Life* (New York: Association Press, 1964), p. 177.

things is only a finalization of the pattern they have already
discerned and endorsed, a forward projection of the prelap-
sarian Paradise which is itself a backward projection of crystallized fantasies. Doctrines, dogmas, the outlines of thought,
paralyze the mind, and persuade it that only a limited reper-
tory of its responses to the world around it are really real,
that all the rest are dreams, chimeras, forms of psychic disturbance. Only thus can the illusion of stability be maintained, and the soul, once taught to fear instability, be kept in
tranquility.

The problem with this attitude is that it may be the very
incarnation of all that is really antireligious and antitheistic.
It divinizes order and stasis, or at least puts them above everything else. It represents nothing more than man's fear of the
unknown, his unwillingness to live in the abyss, to see the
naked face of God, to expose himself completely in the quest
for experience and being.

It is entirely possible that there is more of an essentially
spiritual nature about Henry Miller's posture of radical openness in "Reflections on Writing" than there is about the typical Christian sermon. Miller says that he became a writer out
of no great overriding convictions or ideas, but merely took
one of a number of paths out of the bog or swamp where he
found himself and later discovered that he had *become* that
path. He says,

> I am a man telling the story of his life, a process which ap-
> pears more and more inexhaustible as I go on. Like the world-
> evolution, it is endless. It is a turning inside out, a voyaging
> through X dimensions, with the result that somewhere along
> the way one discovers that what one has to tell is not nearly so
> important as the telling itself. It is this quality about all art
> which gives it a metaphysical hue, which lifts it out of time
> and space and centers or integrates it to the whole cosmic
> process. It is this about art which is "therapeutic": significance,
> purposelessness, infinitude.[19]

19. Henry Miller, *The Wisdom of the Heart* (New York: New Directions,
1960), p. 20.

There is no "goal" for the artist, he says: he merely digs
deeper and deeper into the particular, and, the deeper he
goes, the more he finds that all paths converge, that life has
a great unity, a unity which itself is transcendent or spiritual.
When he first began to write, says Miller, he imitated all the
great writers, especially Nietzsche, Dostoevsky, Hamsun, and
Thomas Mann—and failed.

Finally I came to a dead end, to a despair and desperation
which few men have known, because there was no divorce between myself as writer and myself as man: to fail as a writer
meant to fail as a man. And I failed. I realized that I was
nothing—less than nothing—a minus quantity. It was at this
point, in the midst of the dead Sargasso Sea, so to speak, that
I really began to write. I began from scratch, throwing everything overboard, even those whom I most loved. Immediately
I heard my own voice, I was enchanted: the fact that it was a
separate, distinct, unique voice sustained me. It didn't matter
to me if what I wrote should be considered bad. Good and bad
dropped out of my vocabulary. I jumped with two feet into the
realm of aesthetics, the non-moral, non-ethical, non-utilitarian
realm of art. My life itself became a work of art. I had found
a voice, I was whole again. The experience was very much like
what we read of in connection with the lives of Zen initiates.
My huge failure was like the recapitulation of the experience
of the race: I had to grow foul with knowledge, realize the
futility of everything, smash everything, grow desperate, then
humble, then sponge myself off the slate, as it were, in order
to recover my authenticity. I had to arrive at the brink and
then take a leap in the dark.

I talk now about Reality, but I know there is no getting at
it, leastwise by writing. I learn less and realize more: I learn in
some different, more subterranean way. I acquire more and
more the gift of immediacy. I am developing the ability to
perceive, apprehend, analyze, synthesize, categorize, inform,
articulate—all at once. The structural element of things reveals
itself more readily to my eye. I eschew all clear cut interpreta-
tions: with increasing simplification the mystery heightens.
What I know tends to become more and more unstatable. I
live in certitude, a certitude which is not dependent upon
proofs or faith. I live completely for myself, without the least

egotism or selfishness. . . . I find that there is plenty of room in the world for everybody—great interspatial depths, great ego universes, great islands of repair, for whoever attains to individuality. On the surface, where the historical battles rage, where everything is interpreted in terms of money and power, there may be crowding but life only begins when one drops below the surface, when one gives up the struggle, sinks and disappears from sight. Now I can as easily not write as write: there is no longer any compulsion, no longer any therapeutic aspect to it. Whatever I do is done out of sheer joy: I drop my fruits like a ripe tree. What the general reader or the critic makes of it is not my concern. I am not establishing values: I defecate and nourish. There is nothing more to it.[20]

There is a remarkable sense of humility in this, of discovery and awe and acceptance and joy. It is basically what the protagonists in Greek drama discovered at the end of the play, when humiliation, being carried into earth, into the dirt, resulted finally in a remarkable sense of unity with the cosmos and the gods of the cosmos. It stands in a line of direct descent from the writings of Lawrence. And it is truer to the spirit of what Paul Tillich called "the Protestant principle"—that there are no such things as "sacred authorities, doctrines, and morals," but that an individual must get up fresh every morning, ready to start over again the process of deciding what is right and true for him[21]—than most Protestants would be willing to credit it with being. It is the word of a man who is still open to the magic of existence, who is still discovering the important subterranean rhythms of life in the total creation.

Lawrence was convinced that Western man has simply come to "the cul-de-sac of mind consciousness," a rationalistic dead end beyond which further effort or expenditure is unprofitable, or at least will be so until the nonrational aspects of his being catch up with the expanded intellect. He did not

20. Ibid., pp. 20–22.
21. Cf. Paul Tillich, *The Protestant Era* (Chicago: University of Chicago Press, 1948), p. 226.

deny that mental consciousness is important; on the contrary, he regarded it as having considerable significance to man's nature and functioning. "But mental consciousness," he said, "is not a goal; it is a cul-de-sac."

> It provides us only with endless *appliances* which we can use for the all-too-difficult business of coming to our spontaneous-creative fulness of being. It provides us with means to adjust ourselves to the external universe. It gives us further means for subduing the external, materio-mechanical universe to our great end of creative life. And it gives us plain indications of how to avoid falling into automatism, hints for the *applying* of the will, the loosening of false, automatic fixations, the brave adherence to a profound soul-impulse. This is the use of the mind—a great indicator and instrument. The mind as author and director of life is anathema.[22]

This latter condition, in which the mind is "author and director of life," he opposed with all his might, for he believed it to be the singular evil in modern life. "My great religion," he said, "is belief in the blood, the flesh, as being wiser than the intellect. We can go wrong in our minds. But what our flesh believes and says, is always true. The intellect is only a bit and a bridle."[23]

If this seems to be strong language, we should perhaps take a clearer look at what Lawrence was opposing. There is a caricature of it in Valéry's portrait of the meticulous Monsieur Teste, whose very name is cognate to the French word for "head." Teste is the epitome of what a human being can become when he determines to be a passionless intelligence. He is so rigorously dedicated to the world of ideas and reflection, in fact, that he has nearly ceased to be a person. He never gestures when he speaks, he ignores all personal amenities, he discourses with uncanny accuracy on the very subjects which force most speakers into metaphorical or imprecise lan-

22. D. H. Lawrence, *Psychoanalysis and the Unconscious* (New York: Thomas Seltzer, 1921), pp. 118–19.
23. D. H. Lawrence, *Collected Letters*, ed. Harry T. Moore (New York: Viking Press, 1962), 1: 180.

guage. "How is it possible," asks the narrator who describes him in the first part of the story, "not to feel enthusiasm for a man who never said anything *vague?*"[24] Valéry was himself an incomparably disciplined person. For over forty years he rose at five every morning to record in notes, meditations, and watercolors the subtle changes produced on his consciousness by the rising of the sun. Renouncing poetry as his *métier* because of its "imprecision," he studied omnivorously in mathematics and the sciences, and devoted himself to prose-reflection the way only a serious clinical scientist devotes himself to the rigors, tedium, and small ecstasies of the laboratory. Years later, after Gide had persuaded him to return to poetry, he wrote a new preface to *Teste*. He had written *Teste*, he said, at a time when he was especially drunk with his own will and "subject to strange excesses of insight" into himself, when he seemed to behold things with a particular luminosity and was striving recklessly to penetrate everything with the sheer power of his attention. Now he could see the vast shortcomings of such a character.

> Regard for the sum total of what he can do rules him. He watches himself, he maneuvers, he is unwilling to be maneuvered. He knows only two values, two categories, those of consciousness reduced to its acts: *the possible* and *the impossible*. In this strange head, where philosophy has little credit, where language is always on trial, there is scarcely a thought that is not accompanied by the feeling that it is tentative; there exists hardly more than the anticipation and execution of definite operations. The short, intense life of this brain is spent in supervising the mechanism by which the relations of the known and the unknown are established and organized. It even uses its obscure and transcendent powers in the obstinate pretense that it is an isolated system in which the infinite has no part.[25]

Note the final confession: "It even uses its obscure and transcendent powers"—that is, its power of distancing itself from

24. Paul Valéry, *Monsieur Teste*, trans. Jackson Mathews (New York: McGraw-Hill, 1964), p. 15.
25. Ibid., pp. 6–7.

the thing observed, its power to reflect and analyze—"in the obstinate pretense that it is an isolated system in which the infinite has no part." The words differ from Lawrence's but the notion is the same: mind-consciousness for its own sake is a dead-end street. Teste is a head *decorpitated*.

The intellectual cul-de-sac nevertheless offers some extraordinary literary possibilities for the perceptive writer, and it is these possibilities which Beckett has so deftly and consistently exploited. Many of his characters could easily represent Teste in old age, debilitated in both mind and spirit, and unable to renew himself either by the power of thought or by the power of relationship to a world he has in earlier years condemned because it could not be reduced absolutely to his own design. Professor Kenner, in his brilliant study of Beckett, notes early on, in a chapter on the novel *Malone Dies*, that Beckett manages even to turn the form of the novel itself into a fitting dirge for *homo philosophicus*:

Malone in bed bears curious analogies with Descartes, whose speculations, notoriously detached from the immediate inspection of visible and audible things, were by preference pursued in the same place. Descartes has at some time fixed a good deal of Mr. Beckett's attention. The marks of this are perfectly clear in *The Unnamable*, the protagonist of which knows that he thinks but would like to feel certain that he exists, as well as in *Molloy*, where the body (at first hardly distinguishable from a bicycle) is as clearly a machine as Descartes established it was, though here a machine subject to loss and decay. This Cartesian focus is something more than a pedantic coincidence. The philosophy which has stood behind all subsequent philosophies, and which makes the whole of intelligible reality depend on the mental processes of a solitary man, came into being at about the same time as the curious literary form called the novel, which has since infected all other literary genres. The novel, for all its look of objectivity, is the product of an arduous solitary ordeal: you can sing your poems and arrange to have your plays acted, but all you can do with your novels is write them, alone in a room, assembling what memories you can of experiences you had before your siege in the room com-

menced, all the time secretly perhaps a little ashamed of the
genre you are practicing. How can all these lies be taken seriously, and all this color? Joyce sought to put in everything,
once and for all, and be done with it.[26]

Molloy, Moran, Malone (do the names matter?), lying in bed,
remembering and writing with the stub of a pencil, is the
decrepit embodiment of what philosophical man has come to,
the ghost of vitality, residue of sophistication, valley of dry
bones. Like Camus's Clamence, in *The Fall*, he may even
have a preference for the subjunctive mood; but he has lost
nearly the last semblance of virility and meaning.

For a cameo portrait of this "Cartesian centaur," or thinking man with a bicycle, Beckett has given us Krapp—the clo-
acal name sums it up!—in the brief play *Krapp's Last Tape*.
Here it is really Proust, the author of the multivolume *Remembrance of Things Past*, who is soundly thumped, and not
Descartes, though philosophy comes in for its drubbing too.
Proust, it will be recalled, sought by piling up references to
past events, references stored up in the memory, to create
enough of the aura of an original event to bring that event to
life again, not as the aboriginal event itself but as a new
original event, capable of existing in the present. The mind,
in other words, *created life in a vacuum*, independent of contemporary events and, indeed, of the whole contemporary
world. It was all a kind of shadow-box art, producing the illusion of reality instead of depending on immediate reality
itself. Beckett was obviously enthralled by Proust at one time,
though he struggled against the enthralment, and wrote a
masterly essay on the Frenchman which is still one of the best
pieces ever done on Proust.[27] *Krapp*, written years later,
shows no traces of the struggle: Proust is vanquished, and
almost by a joke.

Krapp sits alone on the stage with a tape-recorder and

26. Hugh Kenner, *Samuel Beckett: A Critical Study* (New York: Grove Press,
1961), pp. 17–18.
27. Samuel Beckett, *Proust* (New York: Grove Press, n.d.). First published in
1931.

dozens of cans of tape, listening to the voices (his own) out
of his past. The machine is thus his memory; and, at least as
far as the conscious mind is concerned, it is far more retentive
than Proust's. Not only have his thoughts been captured on
tape; there are layers upon layers of his thought; whenever
he has laughed or cursed or made additional remarks while
listening to a tape, these additional thoughts or reactions have
been transcribed into the record. Now he appears to be re-
playing the tapes in an effort to find something from his past
capable of supporting his present, and perhaps, thereby, his
future. But the effort is futile. Inevitably, at the end, he col-
lapses in a failure of meaning.

What was Valéry's description of Teste? A "strange head,
where philosophy has little credit, where language is always
on trial, [where] there is scarcely a thought that is not accom-
panied by the feeling that it is tentative"? It could as easily
describe Krapp. He no longer finds any philosophy acceptable. Whenever a segment of tape approaches which promises
to divulge something he once believed or thought, he now
strikes the switch and sends the tape speeding ahead to another subject. For example, this passage:

> Spiritually a year of profound gloom and indigence until
> that memorable night in March, at the end of the jetty, in the
> howling wind, never to be forgotten, when suddenly I saw the
> whole thing. The vision, at last. This I fancy is what I have
> chiefly to record this evening, against the day when my work
> will be done and perhaps no place left in my memory, warm
> or cold, for the miracle that . . . (*hesitates*) . . . for the fire that
> set it alight. What I suddenly saw then was this, that the belief
> I had been going on all my life, namely—(*Krapp switches off
> impatiently, winds tape forward, switches on again*)—great
> granite rocks the foam flying up in the light of the lighthouse
> and the wind-gauge spinning like a propellor, clear to me at
> last that the dark I have always struggled to keep under is in
> reality my most—(*Krapp curses, switches off, winds tape for-
> ward, switches on again*)—unshatterable association until my
> dissolution of storm and night with the light of the under-

standing and the fire—(*Krapp curses louder, switches off, winds tape forward, switches on again*)—my face in her breasts and my hand on her. We lay there without moving. But under us all moved, and moved us, gently, up and down, and from side to side.[28]

The business with the girl—somewhere in a punt on a lake—is the one moment of reality to which Krapp recurs again and again. The rest disgusts him now. Only the touching of flesh remains.

Language, which had once doubtless seemed the very tool of the gods to Krapp, has been permitted to languish. Listening to the tape, his ear catches on a word from an earlier year which he no longer recognizes. The voice on the tape says, ". . . there is of course the house on the canal where mother lay a-dying, in the late autumn, after her long viduity. . . ." Krapp gives a start, and flips the switch. He winds the tape back and replays the segment. "Viduity." It has completely escaped him. He exits, and comes back momentarily with an enormous dictionary, lays it on the table, and looks up the word. Viduity. "State—or condition of being—or remaining—a widow—or widower." But what is the point of keeping the artillery of language polished and ready when the battle of philosophy is over? There was a time when language was "always on trial" with him; now there is not even reason for a trial.

"The feeling that everything is tentative. . . ." Krapp finally picks up the microphone and adds another word to the tape he has just been auditing. "Just been listening to that stupid bastard I took myself for thirty years ago," he says; "hard to believe I was ever as bad as that. Thank God that's all done with anyway."

He pauses.

Then he says, "The eyes she had!"[29]

28. Samuel Beckett, *Krapp's Last Tape and Other Pieces* (New York: Grove Press, n.d.), pp. 20–21.
29. Ibid., p. 24.

The girl, the thing of the flesh, that is the one oasis of meaning in the desert of his mind. He puts on another tape, and listens again to a passage about the girl. When it ends, he sits, staring without motion. The play is over. Really over.

This is the cul-de-sac. This is what it looks like, what it feels like, what it *is* like. This is the life of the mind when it gets out of balance or out of harmony with the other human faculties, when it is given preeminence without major responsibilities to the rest of the body. Man is so cut off from things, from the sensation of the world around him, that he has almost, inadvertently and ironically, become a thing himself, albeit a curious and highly complicated one. In his false and illusory impressions of transcendence, he has become increasingly isolated from everything, until there is no longer anything to sustain him, to feed life into him.

Then it almost seems that things are in league against him. The mind becomes paranoid and imagines that the universe is actively hostile to it. The movements, the political acts, the traffic, the noises, the very furniture in the front parlor (as in Ionesco's *The New Tenant*), are seen as engaged in a gigantic conspiracy to overthrow the mind and establish their own rulership, a rulership which to the mind can only appear as total anarchy. There is no friendliness in anything inanimate. Madness is the only escape.

Lawrence, with a mystical sense of what human wholeness is, sought to redress our worship of the intellect and its powers. He was not really antiphilosophical, as some have charged. He only realized what some philosophers forget, that the mind is a physiological machine and depends for its proper functioning on the remainder of the body and the body's relationship to the universe it exists in. There are currents of life flowing in the universe, Gulf Streams of being, and man is sanest and healthiest when he aligns himself with the flow, not when he sets up some part or all of himself as an obstruction to the flow. One cannot forbear contrasting the account of Monsieur Teste or of the desiccated Krapp with that of the

Brangwen family in this famous passage at the beginning of
Lawrence's *The Rainbow*:

> So the Brangwens came and went without fear of necessity,
> working hard because of the life that was in them, not for want
> of the money. Neither were they thriftless. They were aware of
> the last halfpenny, and instinct made them not waste the peel-
> ing of their apple, for it would help to feed the cattle. But
> heaven and earth was teeming around them, and how should
> this cease? They felt the rush of the sap in spring, they knew
> the wave which cannot halt, but every year throws forward the
> seed to begetting, and, falling back leaves the young-born on
> the earth. They knew the intercourse between heaven and
> earth, sunshine drawn into the breast and bowels, the rain
> sucked up in the daytime, nakedness that comes under the
> wind in autumn, showing the birds' nests no longer worth
> hiding. Their life and interrelations were such; feeling the
> pulse and body of the soil, that opened to their furrow for the
> grain, and became smooth and supple after their ploughing,
> and clung to their feet with a weight that pulled like desire,
> lying hard and unresponsive, when the crops were to be shorn
> away. The young corn waved and was silken, and the lustre
> slid along the limbs of the men who saw it. They took the
> udder of the cows, the cows yielded milk and pulse against the
> hands of the men, the pulse of the blood of the teats of the
> cows beat into the pulse of the hands of the men. They
> mounted their horses, and held life between the grip of their
> knees, they harnessed their horses at the wagon, and, with hand
> on the bridle-rings, drew the heaving of the horses after their
> will.
> In autumn the partridges whirred up, birds in flocks blew
> like spray across the fallow, rooks appeared on the grey, watery
> heavens, and flew cawing into the water. Then the men sat by
> the fire in the house where the women moved about with
> surety, and the limbs and the body of the men were impreg-
> nated with the day, cattle and earth and vegetation and the
> sky, the men sat by the fire and their brains were inert, as their
> blood flowed heavy with the accumulation from the living day.[30]

There is something fundamental, one would almost say *primeval*, about this. The sense of unity it expresses—what F. R.

30. D. H. Lawrence, *The Rainbow* (New York: Viking Press, 1961), pp. 1–2.

Leavis called the "blood-intimacy"—seems paradisical, as though it belonged to a golden age. The imagery is almost totally sexual—intercourse, penetration, suffusion, rhythm, impregnation, flow, mutuality. Man is not cut off from the world of his environment; he moves in profound accord with it, drawing life from it. The rhythms of the seasons, the days, the weather, growth, decay, are his rhythms too. He is not at counterpurposes with life. His rationality has not triumphed at the expense of his balance and wholeness. He is "deeply and sensually in touch with that which can be touched but not known." Childlike, but not childishly, he lives in a perpetual "reign of wonder."

This phrase, "the reign of wonder," which is from Carlyle's *Sartor Resartus*, is also the title of one of the most penetrating studies of American literature ever made. Critic Tony Tanner traces it as a characteristic of the frontier spirit in American letters, where, from Emerson on, it was a "key strategy" of writers. It was there before Emerson, of course, but with him it became crucial, for he was a transcendentalist and a philosopher and, at the same time, a careful observer of nature; he was, in other words, "a man talking metaphysics with his eye glued to the microscope," a man making facts "yield their secret sense." His emphasis was most important for American writers, says Tanner, "because among other things he was continually dragging eyes back to the worth and status of American facts."[31] He made available to future writers of literature in America a whole inventory of materials which had never before enjoyed true respectability. The entire phenomenon of regionalism from Sara Orne Jewett to Jesse Stuart and Wendell Berry has owed much to this opening up of the local and the concrete kind of reality.

What it is about, says Tanner, is seeing with the "naive vision, the innocent eye." The writings of Emerson, Thoreau,

31. Tony Tanner, *The Reign of Wonder: Naivety and Reality in American Literature* (Cambridge: Cambridge University Press, 1965), p. 39.

Whitman, Mark Twain, Sherwood Anderson, Hemingway,
are the products of the *admiring* spirit, the spirit that looks
on in awe and wonder, that really *sees* the world instead of
seeing through it. Tanner draws on Auerbach's *Mimesis* for
a descriptive term. Auerbach distinguishes between *paratactic* style and *hypotactic* style in syntax: the first simply juxta-
poses things without making an effort to relate them and the
second organizes and relates things by a variety of subordinate clauses. The style which best expresses the American
vision, says Tanner, appears to be paratactic. Consider, as a
prime example, the great, rambling catalogues of Whitman.
Hypotactic syntax is much more likely to occur in European
writing where centuries of tradition have resulted in multiple
subordination processes. The American resistance to hier-
archical systems has preserved a more "innocent" approach to
the world. If one is asked to name an American writer who
specialized in subordinate clauses, he is most likely to think
of Henry James, whose constant strategy was to bring the
naive eye into conflict with the social complexities of Anglo-
European life. James was a special kind of entrepreneur at
the meeting point between the cultures. But for the most part
American letters have been characterized by an almost proud
resistance to the "civilized" virtues. Analysis, which is the
European forte, is rejected for beholding. Thus Henry Miller:

> What strikes me now as the most wonderful proof of my
> fitness, or unfitness, for the times is the fact that nothing peo-
> ple were writing or talking about had any real interest for me.
> Only the object haunted me, the separate, detached, insignifi-
> cant *thing*. It might be a part of the human body or a staircase
> in a vaudeville house; it might be a smokestack or a button I
> had found in the gutter. Whatever it was it enabled me to open
> up, to surrender, to attach my signature. . . . I was filled with
> a perverse love of the thing-in-itself—not a philosophic attach-
> ment, but a passionate, desperately passionate hunger, as if in
> this discarded, worthless *thing* which everyone ignored there
> was contained the secret of my own regeneration.[32]

32. Henry Miller, *Tropic of Capricorn* (New York: Grove Press, 1961), p. 54.

One could think of dozens of related passages, in Crane, in Dreiser, in Wolfe, in Jarrell, in Bellow, in Brautigan, though none more insistent of notice perhaps than Hemingway's famous speech about abstract words in *A Farewell to Arms*. The intransigence of the particular runs like a creedal statement through American letters, and flowers at last in one of the very finest of recent poets, Theodore Roethke, whose mind, as Hoffman says, "was drenched in particulars."[33] I cite especially his little poem "Root Cellar," which is representative not only because many of his most splendid compositions trace their relationship to his work in the family greenhouse but because the imagery, impregnate of earth, reminds me somehow of the Brangwen passage from Lawrence.

> Nothing would sleep in that cellar, dank as a ditch,
> Bulbs broke out of boxes hunting for chinks in the dark,
> Shoots dangled and drooped,
> Lolling obscenely from mildewed crates,
> Hung down long yellow evil necks, like tropical snakes.
> And what a congress of stinks!—
> Roots ripe as old bait,
> Pulpy stems, rank, silo-rich,
> Leaf-mold, manure, lime, piled against slippery planks.
> Nothing would give up life:
> Even the dirt kept breathing a small breath.[34]

The special quality about Roethke's verse, which W. D. Snodgrass calls "that anguish of concreteness"[35] and Kenneth Burke a kind of "vegetal radicalism,"[36] led Nathan A. Scott,

33. Frederick J. Hoffman, "Theodore Roethke: The Poetic Shape of Death," *Theodore Roethke: Essays on the Poetry*, ed. Arnold Stein (Seattle: University of Washington Press, 1965), p. 111.
34. Theodore Roethke, *Words for the Wind* (Bloomington: Indiana University Press, 1961), p. 39.
35. W. D. Snodgrass, " 'That Anguish of Concreteness'—Theodore Roethke's Career," in Arnold Stein, *Theodore Roethke*, p. 78.
36. Kenneth Burke, "The Vegetal Radicalism of Theodore Roethke," *Sewanee Review* 58, no. 1 (January-March 1950): 68–108. Cited by Nathan A. Scott, Jr., *The Wild Prayer of Longing: Poetry and the Sacred* (New Haven: Yale University Press, 1971), p. 89.

Jr., to speak of his way of "immanentizing" what is "out there" and of discovering "an engrossing but unfathomable density in the Is-ness of everything that exists, in the mysterious munificence with which even dirt and weeds and garden slugs are indwelt by Being." "So his characteristic mode of predication," Scott continues, "is not the subjunctive or the imperative but the indicative, and it is his deep piety toward all the concrete, tangible things of earth that fills his poetry with exclamations. He makes us feel that he was a man who was always prepared to cry out with Landor, 'Good God, the violets!' "[37]

The attitude of wonder was got at differently, but no less significantly, by Wallace Stevens, for whom the finite meant not only the dirt and weeds and garden slugs but the inisolable relationship of these when first encountered by the human eye. As Monet and the impressionists had reconceived the visual technique of the artist, Stevens wanted to reinstruct the poetic eye, to teach it to take in the glory of the whole which the eye normally dismisses as soon as it has managed to focus on separate items within its field. To accomplish this, he worked to develop a kind of artificial speech whose main technique consisted of washing out definitive lines and allowing impressions to flow into one another, creating conjoint impressions instead of discrete ones, totalities instead of individualities. Consciousness for most persons is a matter of individuating: we enter a room and immediately set about discerning what is in it, how things are arranged, how they may be separated and managed. We ignore that split second of apprehension when the objects before us have not coagulated into familiar shapes and objects; it is a hallucinatory half-state to be got beyond, a filmy moment to be despatched by the blinking of the eyes. But Stevens sought to freeze this more dynamic or fluid state of being in his poetry, to hold it fast and permit the senses to return to it, to feel it at greater length, to appropriate it. Consider, for instance, the first

37. Scott, *Wild Prayer of Longing*, pp. 102–3.

stanza of "Sunday Morning," which many critics assess as his finest composition:

> Complacencies of the peignoir, and late
> Coffee and oranges in a sunny chair,
> And the green freedom of a cockatoo
> Upon a rug mingle to dissipate
> The holy hush of ancient sacrifice.
> She dreams a little, and she feels the dark
> Encroachment of that old catastrophe,
> As a calm darkens among water-lights.
> The pungent oranges and bright, green wings
> Seem things in some procession of the dead,
> Winding across wide water, without sound.
> The day is like wide water, without sound,
> Stilled for the passing of her dreaming feet
> Over the seas, to silent Palestine,
> Dominion of the blood and sepulchre.[38]

The images, while sufficient to evoke recognition, are not frozen, but melt into one another for a composite effect. What can one make of phrases such as "complacencies of the peignoir," "green freedom of a cuckatoo," "holy hush of ancient sacrifice," "that old catastrophe," "calm darkens among water-lights," "day . . . like wide water, without sound"? Singly, very little if anything. But together they become a kind of fluid mosaic, subtle, delicate, blending softly into a whole, so that the whole, not its parts, is important.

The apprehension of this whole was, to Stevens, a transcendent act of the mind, a moment of vision in which the reality behind or beyond the existences of discrete or individual objects is grasped and exalted. He called this reality "major reality," to distinguish it from the reality of mere haecceities or specific things. In this sense, he was an idealist. Yet he resisted the Platonic philosophy of idealism that the mind can exist in itself, irrespective of hard facts, and de-

38. Wallace Stevens, "Sunday Morning," *The Collected Poems of Wallace Stevens* (New York: Alfred A. Knopf, 1954).

velop its concepts and categories either apart from those facts or in triumph over them. In a paper on Marianne Moore's poem "He 'Digesteth Harde Yron'," he referred approvingly to an essay by H. D. Lewis entitled "On Poetic Truth":

> Mr. Lewis says that poetry has to do with matter that is foreign and alien. It is never familiar to us in the way in which Plato wished the conquests of the mind to be familiar. On the contrary its function, the need which it meets and which has to be met in some way in every age that is not to become decadent or barbarous, is precisely this contact with reality as it impinges upon us from outside, the sense that we can touch and feel a solid reality which does not wholly dissolve itself into the conceptions of our own minds.[39]

He denied the existence of a gnostic reality, a reality which can be known apart from the itemized facts of our existence; and, on the other hand, he resisted the temptation to find reality in the facts themselves, saying, "No fact is a bare fact, no individual fact is a universe in itself."[40] What he spoke for, like Emerson and Thoreau before him, was the reality "of or within or beneath the surface of reality," a reality which *becomes* reality in tension with the mind knowing it, the person perceiving it. This is to give the world its due as the arena of human experience, as the source of all the data we have, without accepting absorption into it, without resigning human consciousness and metaphysical distance from it. "The greatest poverty," said Stevens in "Esthétique du Mal," "is not to live/ In a physical world."[41]

Admittedly, "major reality" for Stevens is not the same thing as Tillich's "ultimate reality"; it is much more pagan, much more devoid of philosophical and theological freight. Yet there is a certain complementariness in the two concepts.

39. Wallace Stevens, *The Necessary Angel* (New York: Vintage Books, 1951). p. 96.
40. Wallace Stevens, *Opus Posthumous*, ed. Samuel F. Morse (New York: Alfred A. Knopf, 1957), p. 213.
41. Wallace Stevens, "Esthétique du Mal," *Transport to Summer* (New York: Alfred A. Knopf, 1942).

Stevens plumps for the necessary sensual experience without which we are not really men of our world, not really receptors in a creation fairly bursting with miracles of color, sight, sound, motion, and so on. Tillich, on the other hand, fully sympathetic to this need for immersion in the sensory and the existential, reminds us that there is yet another element to our experience, something intangible which can never finally shape itself to the merely sensual, but transcends the sensual and tries to make meaning of it. We are irresponsible in our religion when we fail to live fully in the world, continually open to the stimuli of the created order; and we are irresponsible to the world itself when we immerse ourselves in sensuality and lose the perspective of transcendence. The world then becomes tedious, boring, threatening, without the palliation of another dimension seen as breaking in upon it, or latent in it; and God, conceptualized and abstracted too far from the world as environment, becomes lifeless, the pale shadow of thought without substance. The two views require each other, quite desperately, in the consciousness of man.

Tanner's assessment of the American experience as a whole, seen through its literary expression, is that the paratactical vision, the naïve and largely uncritical way of seeing the world, has actually kept alive in that experience a sense of wonderment or awe which, while it is certainly not missing in European literature, has nowhere else assumed the proportions of a major tradition. One immediately suspects, of course, that all of this has something to do with the nature of frontier life and its effect upon the consciousness, and, essentially, the same phenomenon noted so memorably by R. W. B. Lewis in his book *The American Adam*.[42] Both studies tend to isolate for emphasis "a renewed and lasting interest in the child" in American letters, not only as "an uncomprehending focus of pathos" (as was often the case in the Euro-

42. R. W. B. Lewis, *The American Adam: Innocence, Tragedy, and Tradition in the Nineteenth Century* (Chicago: University of Chicago Press, 1968).

pean tradition of the eighteenth and nineteenth centuries) but as "a superior witness of the world." Says Tanner, "When Sherwood Anderson, for instance, writes: 'A man, if he is any good, never gets over being a boy' or when Saul Bellow asserts 'It's hard in our time to be as naive as one would like,' the accent and emphasis is distinctly American and does not involve an idealization of mere immaturity but rather a feeling for some valuable unencumbered simplicity of response."[43] Tanner goes on to suggest that the American preference for the vernacular is somehow related to this emphasis on naïveté, as though unstudied and even unlearned speech were more capable of discovering the world and its significance than language rendered subtle by philosophy and philology.

A winsome paradigm, in European literature and not American, is the case of Camus's M. Clamence in *The Fall*, who while admitting his own preference for the subjunctive mood expresses undisguised admiration for the simian grunts and vocables of the Mexico City's bartender, and, at the same time, for the latter's uncomplicated vision of reality. And a related phenomenon is the Dadaist-Surrealist movement with its theories of the relationship of wordplay and linguistic freedom to genuine creativity. To induce a sense of this freedom, the followers of Hugo Ball and André Breton often played children's games and attempted to reenter the fantasy world of childhood. At such times they wrote or spoke whatever entered their heads without any attempt at editing or monitoring it. The early studies of Freud and other Viennese psychoanalysts appears to substantiate the significance of this unstructured, paratactical speech: it eluded the tyrannical patterns imposed upon thought through the centuries and permitted creative and innovative response. Breton, who in his *Manifestoes* gave explicit instructions for "automatic" writing, had high praise for the "poet" Robert Desnos, who apparently could fall into a trance whenever he liked and

43. Tanner, *Reign of Wonder*, p. 12.

begin to speak unrelated words and phrases. "Desnos," said Breton, *"speaks Surrealist at will."*[44]

Setting aside the question of how American literature is to be characterized, let us speculate for a moment on the interrelationship of these various matters, childhood, play, and language on one hand, and, on the other, the matter of sensuality. To what extent, if any, are they mutually involved in man's attempt to "get at," to perceive, to know his environment? There is no doubt, in a passage like the account of Lawrence's Brangwen family cited earlier, of a conspiracy of language and feeling, words and flesh. The passage veritably writhes with terms which are sexually suggestive or connotative. Men, animals, and land are all joined in a single rhythm, a single pulsating current. But is there a less manipulative language, one not so heavily programmed to do its work of evangelizing, which by its apparent playfulness brings us into touch with the world in new and unexpected ways? Johan Huizinga did not hesitate, in *Homo Ludens*, to link "playing" and "knowing" in religious ritual, especially in such particular instances as the enigmatic questions of the Vedic hymns and the riddle-contests of many primitive religions; he observed, in fact, that in a majority of the world's religions, play-language is regarded much more positively than serious language.[45] Is this because religions are generally otherworldly and play is a means of *escaping* present reality, or is play-association actually a method of permitting the world to be the world, to make its entry without restriction, and so of *embracing* the world in worship? Huizinga, who proceeds from his discussion of "playing" and "knowing" to a discussion of "playing" and *"poiesis,"* or "playing" and "making," obviously regards the latter to be the case; that is, playing is essential to knowing the world which becomes the stuff of "making" or philosophy. Is such an insight borne out in

44. André Breton, *Manifestoes of Surrealism*, trans. Richard Seaver and Helen R. Lane (Ann Arbor: University of Michigan Press, 1969), pp. 29–30.
45. Johan Huizinga, *Homo Ludens: A Study of the Play Element in Culture* (Boston: Beacon Press, 1965), pp. 105–18.

literature generally, and, if it is, how is it in turn related to perceiving or knowing God?

We cannot speak of "playing" and "knowing" without referring almost immediately to Joyce, whose singular literary method was to luxuriate in short passages, even sentences, until they had become fecundated with associations and the associations were themselves imbedded in the final draft of the passage. Take the merest phrase, "his penisolate war," which occurs in the second paragraph of *Finnegans Wake*: both geographical and sexual imagery, as well as a suggestion of individuation or loneliness, are caught in a single conglomerate word. Where Pound employed what he called "ideogrammic" representation, evoking images by the juxtaposition of certain words and phrases, Joyce went a step further and packed the images into individual words, so that the reader is carried, often for reasons which escape him, into the shimmering depths of a kind of imagaic reverberation, and experiences, partly subliminally, the subtle undulations of references to all sorts of mythical, historical, sexual, psychological, and religious matters. Every word becomes a "portmanteau" of associations, wafting the reader into a larger and larger universe of experience and revelation. This is, in a sense, the opposite of naïve language; it requires all that the reader can possibly bring to it in terms of cultural and psychological sophistication, and then some. It assumes of course that reality is much more than mere current experience, or that current experience somehow involves the totality of man's past, both individually and collectively, as well as his present awareness or appropriation of the past. The point is, however, that regardless of Joyce's vast and profound erudition he was essentially after the same thing as American vernacular writers, namely, a fuller discovery of man's world and how he inhabits it. Play was part of his methodology; without taking the child's part, as so many American authors have chosen to do, he tricked the mind's censors and more closely approximated the paratactical vision.

Henry Miller provides an interesting contrast to Joyce, eschewing compactness, the "portmanteau" approach, for voluminousness and verbosity. One imagines him, instead of working for days on a single sentence, getting a little wine in him and dashing off a dozen pages at a sitting, punctuating some marvelous rhetorical flight only for the mundane necessity of retiring to the bathroom to urinate. Joyce's freedom was in the mind—he ruminated, studied, free-associated, and compressed his language. Miller, on the other hand, found his freedom in the writing itself, in letting go on paper, in the abandonment of discipline. His logomancy is in long, brilliant passages which erupt as erratically as volcanoes and yet by their sheer effusiveness and power pace his entire novels with interest and vitality. Here is an example from *Tropic of Cancer*:

> Boris hands me money to buy liquor. Going for the liquor I am already intoxicated. I know just how I'll begin when I get back to the house. Walking down the street it commences, the grand speech inside me that's gurgling like Mrs. Wren's loose laugh. Seems to me she had a slight edge on already. Listens beautifully when she's tight. Coming out of the wine shop I hear the urinal gurgling. Everything is loose and splashy. I want Mrs. Wren to listen. . . .
>
> Boris is rubbing his hands again. Mr. Wren is still stuttering and spluttering. I have a bottle between my legs and I'm shoving the corkscrew in. Mrs. Wren has her mouth parted expectantly. The wine is splashing between my legs, the sun is splashing through the bay window, and inside my veins there is a bubble and splash of a thousand crazy things that commence to gush out of me now pell-mell. I'm telling them everything that comes to mind, everything that was bottled up inside me and which Mrs. Wren's loose laugh has somehow released. With that bottle between my legs and the sun splashing through the window I experience once again the splendor of those miserable days when I first arrived in Paris, a bewildered, poverty-stricken individual who haunted the streets like a ghost at a banquet. Everything comes back to me in a rush—the toilets that wouldn't work, the prince who shined my shoes,

the Cinema Splendide where I slept on the patron's overcoat, the bars in the window, the feeling of suffocation, the fat cockroaches, the drinking and carousing that went on between times, Rose Cannaque and Naples dying in the sunlight. Dancing the streets on an empty belly and now and then calling on strange people—Madame Delorme, for instance. How I ever got to Madame Delorme's, I can't imagine any more. But I got there, got inside somehow, past the butler, past the maid with her little white apron, got right inside the palace with my corduroy trousers and my hunting jacket—and not a button on my fly. Even now I can taste again the golden ambiance of that room where Madame Delorme sat upon a throne in her mannish rig, the goldfish in the bowls, the maps of the ancient world, the beautifully bound books; I can feel again her heavy hand resting upon my shoulder, frightening me a little with her heavy Lesbian air. More comfortable down below in that thick stew pouring into the Gare St. Lazare, the whores in the doorways, seltzer bottles on every table; a thick tide of semen flooding the gutters. Nothing better between five and seven than to be pushed around in that throng, to follow a leg or a beautiful bust, to move alone with the tide and everything whirling in your brain. A weird sort of contentment in those days. No appointments, no invitations for dinner, no program, no dough. The golden period, when I had not a single friend. Each morning the dreary walk to the American Express, and each morning the inevitable answer from the clerk. Dashing here and there like a bedbug, gathering butts now and then, sometimes furtively, sometimes brazenly; sitting down on a bench and squeezing my guts to stop the gnawing, or walking through the Jardin de Tuileries and getting an erection looking at the dumb statues. Or wandering along the Seine at night, wandering and wandering, and going mad with the beauty of it, the trees leaning to, the broken images in the water, the rush of the current under the bloody lights of the bridges, the women sleeping in doorways, sleeping on newspapers, sleeping in the rain; everywhere the musty porches of the cathedrals and beggars and lice and old hags full of St. Vitus' dance; pushcarts stacked up like wine barrels in the side streets, the smell of berries in the market place and the old church surrounded with vegetables and blue arc lights, the gutters slippery with garbage and women in satin pumps staggering through the filth and vermin at the end of an all-night souse. The Place St.

Sulpice, so quiet and deserted, where toward midnight there came every night the woman with the busted umbrella and the crazy veil; every night she slept there on a bench under her torn umbrella, the ribs hanging down, her dress turning green, her bony fingers and the odor of decay oozing from her body; and in the morning I'd be sitting there myself, taking a quiet snooze in the sunshine, cursing the goddamned pigeons gathering up the crumbs everywhere. St. Sulpice! The fat belfries, the garish posters over the door, the candles flaming inside. The Square so beloved of Anatole France, with that drone and buzz from the altar, the splash of the fountain, the pigeons cooing, the crumbs disappearing like magic and only a dull rumbling in the hollow of the guts. Here I would sit day after day thinking of Germaine and that dirty little street near the Bastille where she lived, and that buzz-buzz going on behind the altar, the buses whizzing by, the sun beating down into the asphalt and the asphalt working into me and Germaine, into the asphalt and all Paris in the big fat belfries.[46]

This passage reflects the "gift of immediacy" of which Miller speaks in *The Wisdom of the Heart.* "I never hope to embrace the whole," he says, "but merely to give in each separate fragment, each work, the feeling of the whole as I go on, because I am digging deeper and deeper into life, digging deeper and deeper into past and future. With the endless burrowing a certitude develops which is greater than faith or belief. I become more and more indifferent to my fate, as writer, and more and more certain of my destiny as man."[47] Again:

A man is revealed in his style, the language which he has created for himself. To the man who is pure at heart I believe that everything is as clear as a bell, even the most esoteric scripts. For such a man there is always mystery, but the mystery is not mysterious, it is logical, natural, ordained, and implicitly accepted. Understanding is not a piercing of the mystery, but an acceptance of it, a living blissfully with it, in it, through

46. Henry Miller, *Tropic of Cancer* (New York: Grove Press, 1961), pp. 13–15.
47. Miller, *Wisdom of the Heart*, p. 20.

and by it. I would like my words to flow along in the same way that the world flows along, a serpentine movement through incalculable dimensions, axes, latitudes, climates, conditions. I accept *a priori* my inability to realize such an ideal. It does not bother me in the least. In the ultimate sense, the world itself is pregnant with failure, is the perfect manifestation of imperfection, of the consciousness of failure. In the realization of this, failure is itself eliminated. Like the primal spirit of the universe, like the unshakable Absolute, the One, the All, the creator, i.e., the artist, expresses himself by and through imperfection. It is the stuff of life, the very sign of livingness. One gets nearer to the heart of truth, which I suppose is the ultimate aim of the writer, in the measure that he ceases to struggle, in the measure that he abandons the will.[48]

There is the playfulness by which Miller makes himself available to the world and, conversely, the world to himself, and by which finally he transcends both in an apprehension of the Absolute. "An apocalyptic comedian," someone has called him.[49] It is not a bad description. "I don't say that God is one grand laugh," he says in *Tropic of Capricorn*; "I say that you've got to laugh hard before you can get anywhere near God. My whole aim in life is to get near to God, that is, to get nearer to myself."[50] What was Lawrence's phrase, "deeply and sensually in touch"? Few would argue that Miller is sensually in touch, but many would question whether he is deeply so. I myself would be hard put, I think, to name anyone who apprehends either the world or God more mystically and directly. The only name that comes to mind, and he is dead now, is Thomas Merton.

Nor can one ignore the drug cult when dealing with sensuality, either in life or in letters. It too is a way of eluding the censors, of returning to primitive conditions, of telescoping myth and psyche, of running free and barefooted in the world

48. Ibid., p. 23.
49. Kingsley Widmer, *Henry Miller* (New York: Twayne Publishers, 1963), p. 17.
50. Miller, *Tropic of Capricorn*, p. 305.

of sensory experience. As Masters and Houston have shown conclusively by their empirical studies, one of the most verifiable data associated with the use of drugs is a heightened sensitivity to the entire sensory context.[51] And the corresponding sense of mystical awareness, of transcendent unity in the cosmos, has become the ambitious study of numerous theologians and phenomenologists. It is perhaps too easy to call the sense of unity God; but it is not easy, on the other hand, to dissociate the sense of unity from more traditional forms of mystical apprehension of the deity.

There is a kind of immediacy, of direct apprehension, in the writings of the current drug culture, of, say, Kerouac and Kesey and Brautigan, which renders academic and meretricious any distinction between religious mysticism and psychedelic ecstasy. Here is a passage from the last chapter of Brautigan's *A Confederate General from Big Sur:*

> The Pacific Ocean rolled to its inevitable course: our bodies at the edge with Lee Mellon rolling dope. He handed some to Elaine. She really went at it, and then she handed it to me. I gave it to Elizabeth, who was like a Greek dance, forgotten in Modern Times.
>
> We smoked five or six chunks of dope and then the ocean began to come in on us in a different manner: I mean, slow and light itself.
>
> I looked over at Elizabeth. She was sitting on a white rock, the wind lighting the end of her red banner. She stared out at the ocean with her head in her hands. Lee Mellon was lying flat on his back, sprawled flung out on the rough sand.
>
> Elaine stared at the waves that were breaking like ice cube trays out of a monk's tooth or something like that. Who knows? I don't know.
>
> I was staring at the three of them, high on their earthly presence and my relationship to the presence. I felt very strange and confused inside.[52]

51. Cf. R. E. L. Masters and Jean Houston, *The Varieties of Psychedelic Experience* (New York: Dell Publishing Co., 1967), pp. 7–13.
52. Richard Brautigan, *A Confederate General from Big Sur* (New York: Grove Press, 1964), p. 154.

Elaine draws him aside. They sit down among the white peb-
bles and the sand and the flies further along the beach. She
wants to make love, and undresses both of them. But he can't
get an erection and it doesn't work. It is all like a fantasy in
slow motion. Then Brautigan provides five possible endings,
hinting at 186,000 more. One reads: "A seagull flew over us,
its voice running with the light, its voice passing historically
through songs of gentle color. We closed our eyes and the
bird's shadow was in our ears."[53] The point is, it doesn't matter how the novel ends. The world *is*—it has Is-ness—what
Meister Eckhardt called *Istigkeit*. The vision is beatific, like
Dante's at the end of his quest for Paradise. The synesthesia
is absolutely natural in a moment of ecstasy. And the sense of
presence, of "earthly presence," of "relationship to the presence," predominates.

In each of these instances—Joyce, Miller, Brautigan—and
in many others which might be adduced on the spectrum
from Lawrence to the present, there is evidence of a kind of
spiritual perception in and through the materialities and particularities of the world itself. Robbe-Grillet aside—I am not
yet sure how he is to be dealt with, only that he *must* be dealt
with—there is in the confrontation with world or earth or
intransigent reality something beyond a merely *chosiste* way
of apprehending it, something beyond a flatly clinical and
scientific series of data or impressions. There is a sense of
something vital in it, something spirited or spiritual, something impregnating it with meaning and yet, withal, to come
back to Hoffman's term, "transcending" it, adding up to
more than the sum of its parts, and imbuing the parts with
wonder and significance because it does. There is no easy way
to describe it, and certainly no final way. It is felt or not felt,
and within either of those instances only an insufficient case
may be made. But the mode of playfulness, surrender, or
abandonment appears to have much to do with an invitation

53. Ibid., p. 159.

to feeling it, and to realizing what Nathan A. Scott, Jr., calls "the very essence of the sacramental principle—namely, that nothing may be a sacrament unless everything is, at bottom, sacramental, and that ours may be considered to be a sacramental universe because, in its every aspect and dimension, it is instinct with that which appears to be *for* man rather than *against* him—which is none other than Being itself."[54]

Realizing the sacramental nature of the universe, the fundamental unity of all that is, is crucially important. Lawrence knew this. He recognized the sterility and arrogance to which mind-consciousness had brought the Christian faith by the end of the nineteenth century, and he set himself against this situation with all his power as an artist. But he also saw the destructiveness of mere passion let loose without aim or relationship. The answer to puritanism was not libertinism, any more than the answer to libertinism is puritanism. In his novel *The Kangaroo* he expressed a concept which is at the heart of all his writings: it is about what he called the "God-passion," a sensually religious passion which somehow holds other human passions in creative and beneficent tension. He had dealt in the narrative with various passions, especially the passion for political life and the passion for money, which he believed lay behind the other passion, and turned finally to talking about love. Being more realistic than most preachers who talk of love, however, he indicated even the inadequacy of that passion. Because of what he called "the inevitable necessity of each individual to react away from any other individual, at certain times," he declared human love to be, even at its best, a relative passion and not an absolute one. And yet, he said, the human heart must have an absolute, for it is one of the conditions of being human. What shall it be?

The only thing is the God who is the source of all passion. Once go down before the God-passion and human passions take

54. Scott, *Wild Prayer of Longing*, pp. 117–18.

their right rhythm. But human love without the God-passion
always kills the thing it loves. Men and women are virtually
killing each other with the love-will now. What would it be
when mates, or comrades, broke down in their absolute love
and trust? Because, without the polarized God-passion to hold
them stable at the centre, break down they would. With no
deep God who is the source of all passion and life to hold them
separate and yet sustained in accord, the loving comrades
would smash one another, and smash all love, all feeling as
well.[55]

This notion of a God who holds things apart as well as together is articulated again in *The Rainbow,* where Lawrence
described the secret strength of Lydia Brangwen, the Polish
widow whom Tom Brangwen married because her foreign-
ness fascinated him.

> She had some beliefs somewhere, never defined. She had
> been brought up a Roman Catholic. She had gone to the
> Church of England for protection. The outward form was a
> matter of indifference to her. Yet she had some fundamental
> religion. It was as if she worshipped God as a mystery, never
> seeking in the least to define what He was.
> And inside her, the subtle sense of the Great Absolute
> wherein she had her being was very strong. The English dogma
> never reached her: the language was too foreign. Through it
> all she felt the great Separator who held life in His hands,
> gleaming, imminent, terrible, the Great Mystery, immediate
> beyond all telling.
> She shone and gleamed to the Mystery, Whom she knew
> through all her senses, she glanced with strange, mystic super-
> stitions that never found expression in the English language,
> never mounted to thought in English. But so she lived, within
> a potent, sensuous belief that included her family and con-
> tained her destiny.
> To this she had reduced her husband. He existed with her
> entirely indifferent to the general values of the world. Her very
> ways, the very mark of her eyebrows were symbols and indica-
> tion to him. There, on the farm with her, he lived through a

55. D. H. Lawrence, *The Kangaroo.* Cited by Leavis, *D. H. Lawrence: Novelist,* pp. 65–66.

mystery of life and death and creation, strange, profound ecstasies and incommunicable satisfactions, of which the rest of
the world knew nothing; which made the pair of them apart
and respected in the English village, for they were also well-
to-do.[56]

Formal belief or doctrine meant nothing to her; in fact, it
seemed to detract from her enthusiasm. She became an assid-
uous churchgoer, says Lawrence: "But the *language* meant
nothing to her; it seemed false. She hated to hear things expressed, put into words. Whilst the religious feelings were
inside her they were passionately moving. In the mouth of the
clergyman, they were false, indecent."[57] The Mystery which
unifies life in the depths of being is essentially nameless and
unthinkable; it pervades all that is and yet has a way of gathering itself beyond all that is; it far transcends the power of
speech or formulization.

There is a reliable clue to Lawrence's feeling, I believe, in
his short novel *The Fox*. It is in the description of the dead
fox, which has had some mysterious but undefinable relation
to Ellen March but has been shot by Henry Grenfel, the
willful young man who has come to live with her and Banford. March and Banford have gone out, first thing in the
morning, to see the fox, which was shot in the night.

> March said nothing, but stood with her foot trailing aside,
> one hip out; her face was pale and her eyes big and black,
> watching the dead animal that was suspended upside down.
> White and soft as snow his belly: white and soft as snow. She
> passed her hand softly down it. And his wonderful black-
> glinted brush was full and frictional, wonderful. She passed
> her hand down this also, and quivered. Time after time she
> took the full fur of that thick tail between her fingers, and
> passed her hand slowly downwards. Wonderful, sharp, thick,
> splendour of a tail. And he was dead! She pursed her lips, and
> her eyes went black and vacant. Then she took the head in her
> hand.

56. Lawrence, *The Rainbow*, pp. 98–99.
57. Ibid., p. 101.

Henry was sauntering up, so Banford walked rather pointedly away. March stood there bemused, with the head of the
fox in her hand. She was wondering, wondering, wondering
over his long, fine muzzle. For some reason it reminded her of
a spoon for a spatula. She felt she could not understand it. The
beast was a strange beast to her, incomprehensible, out of her
range. Wonderful silver whiskers he had, like ice-threads. And
pricked ears with hair inside. But that long, long, slender
spoon of a nose!—and the marvellous white teeth beneath! It
was to thrust forward and bite with, deep, deep, deep into the
living prey, to bite and bite the blood.

"He's a beauty, isn't he?" said Henry, standing by.

"Oh yes, he's a fine big fox. I wonder how many chickens
he's responsible for," she replied.

"A good many. Do you think he's the same one you saw in
the summer?"

"I should think very likely he is," she replied.

He watched her, but he could make nothing of her. Partly
she was so shy and virgin, and partly she was so grim, matter-
of-fact, shrewish. What she said seemed to him so different
from the look of her big, queer, dark eyes.

"Are you going to skin him?" she asked.

"Yes, when I've had breakfast, and got a board to peg him
on."

"My word, what a strong smell he's got! Pooo. It'll take some
washing off one's hands. I don't know why I was so silly as to
handle him." And she looked at her right hand, that had
passed down his belly and along his tail, and had even got a
tiny streak of blood from one dark place in his fur.

"Have you seen the chickens when they smell him, how
frightened they are?" he said.

"Yes, aren't they!"

"You must mind you don't get some of his fleas."

"Oh, fleas!" she replied, nonchalant.

Later in the day she saw the fox's skin nailed flat on a board,
as if crucified. It gave her an uneasy feeling.[58]

Something exists between March and the fox, something inexplicable but nevertheless deep and real. Through him she

58. D. H. Lawrence, *The Fox* in *The Portable D. H. Lawrence* (New York:
Viking Press, 1947).

is in touch with things which can be "touched but not known"—with the wild glory of nature and the elements and a hidden realm of life. And then the description of the magnificent pelt is driven deeper and connected to something else, the crucifixion of Christ. The "tiny streak of blood from one dark place in his fur" recalls the riven side, and the cruciform skin the cross. Natural world and religious symbolism are riveted together, beautifully, compellingly, unforgettably. This is the way it was for Lawrence, how the God-passion was related to all human passions. Sensuality for him did not mean throwing over religion but recovering it in its blood stage, its prerationalistic stage, when what was celebrated in the Communion was in rhythm with floods and tides and seasons of the soul. It meant being united feverishly and compulsively to the world where the grandeur of God, as Hopkins put it, "gathers to a greatness, like the ooze of oil/ Crushed" and will "flame out, like shining from shook foil,"[59] and where, as Maud Bodkin had it,[60] the life-force itself is equivalent to resurrection.

Is this merely a residual theism in Lawrence, one asks, a carry-over from earlier patterns of transcendence which he would have forsworn had he lived into the so-called post-Christian era and been able to purge his system of theological biases? Or is an emphasis on the God-passion hard, tough realism, an honest view and a sound appraisal of the human situation? I am inclined to say it is the latter that it is a good word of advice to all socialist utopians. Man is not man without passion; yet he is most indefensible against his own passions. Only the God-passion—the remembrance of a wildly transcendent dimension in the midst of all else—is able to keep our discreter passions in bounds and in relationship, and to approximate a sense of meaning or direction in exis-

59. Gerard Manley Hopkins, "God's Grandeur," *Selected Poems and Prose* (Baltimore: Penguin Books, 1953), p. 27.
60. Maud Bodkin, *Archetypal Patterns in Poetry: Psychological Studies of Imagination* (London: Oxford University Press, 1963), pp. 60–61.

tence. Otherwise the sheer physicality of life becomes as op-
pressive as an overly dominant psychicality, and we feel with
Roethke that

> Too much reality can be a dazzle, a surfeit;
> Too close immediacy an exhaustion:
> As when the door swings open in a florist's storeroom—
> The rush of smells strikes like a cold fire, the
>   throat freezes,
> And we turn back to the heat of August,
> Chastened.[61]

As Sam Keen was at pains to show us in *Apology for Wonder*,[62] there is something a little pathological about either the
Dionysian man or the Apollonian man *in extremis*: one is
too foolishly exuberant and ignorant of the tenacity of evil in
the world, and the other is too stupidly responsible and ignorant of wonder and miracle. What Keen called for was *homo
tempestivus*, a man of the times, of any season, who could
bring the virtues of both ancient gods into balance in his life.
And this, it seems to me, is precisely what Lawrence was
about: a man who feels, and feels deeply, whose sense of
worldly realities survives and triumphs beyond all the re-
pressions history and technology have practiced upon it; and
yet a man who does not idolize his feeling, or regard it in and
of itself as the be-all or end-all of his existence, but who, because he is a man of acuter sensibilities, turns the healthiness
of his feelings back upon the world to accept it, redeem it,
purchase it, endow it, not necessarily with human qualities,
but with such qualities as make a fuller humanity more possible within it. It is a little like what Hopkins called "in-
scape": the joining together of the world that is given with
the way of seeking that is deeply obliged or committed, so
that the tension at the center, the delicious, inexpressible, al-

61. Theodore Roethke, "The Abyss," *The Far Field: Last Poems* (New York:
Anchor Books, 1971), p. 52.
62. Sam Keen, *Apology for Wonder* (New York: Harper and Row, 1969).

most unbearable Godpull upon things, deepens life and makes it more humane at the same time that it unites it more completely to the natural cosmos. "The dearest freshness deep down things" is seen to be indissolubly linked to the presence of "the Holy Ghost over the bent/World brood[ing] with warm breast and with ah! bright wings."[63]

It is a word secular man needs to hear. Without it, *things* get out of hand. As in a play by Beckett or Ionesco, they madden the characters with their exaggerated opacity and obtuseness; they weigh upon souls like witchpresses until souls expire or flee. Or, in men lacking some saving residue of civilization, they are turned to pornographic uses, and revulse by omnipresence. And it is a word the church needs to hear—the church that has surrendered spatiality for spirituality, that has lost the ability to inhabit the earth. "The last thing to be realized," says Norman O. Brown, "is the incarnation."[64] This is hard for the church to understand; it had assumed that everything *began* with the incarnation and that now we are going in the opposite direction. But no: "The last mystery to be unveiled is the union of humanity and divinity *in the body*."[65] The garden of Eden lies before us, not behind us. Fulfillment is finally carnal.

63. Hopkins, "God's Grandeur."
64. Brown, *Love's Body*, p. 221.
65. Ibid. My italics.

IV.

Reaping the Whirlwind:
God in the Literature of the Black Experience

There are striking differences between current black
writings and the most significant white literature of our time.
At the substantive level, the experience which informs black
authorship tends to be more elemental and less diffuse. It has
a sociopolitical character, and, excepting the philosophical
traditions which lay behind them, is more akin to writings
related to the American War of Independence or to the
French Revolution than to the intellectually transpolitical
concerns of a Beckett or a Henry Miller. Much of it, for that
reason, is autobiographical in the direct and primary sense of
the word. That is, the details of the author's life, of his external circumstances, are not merely the stuff of philosophical
rumination, history transmuted into thought; they are crucially important, on the contrary, as unadorned documenta-
tion, as the authentic record of a way of life and of the
revolution that is changing that way of life. Black authors
who do not deal directly and unsophisticatedly with the facts,
but have achieved some aesthetic and philosophical distance
from the material, appear strangely incongruent in any discussion of the black experience. They have been assimilated.
They no longer speak as black. They are persons without color.
There is an unmistakable key to the black attitude toward
writing in the prose-poem called "Black Art" by LeRoi Jones
who has recently adopted the name, Imamu Amiri Baraka:

Poems are bullshit unless they are teeth or
trees or lemons piled on a step.

. . . .

We want live words of the hip world
live flesh and coursing blood. Hearts
Brains Souls splintering fire. We want
poems like fists

. . . .

We want "poems that kill."
Assassin poems, poems that shoot guns.
Poems that wrestle cops into alleys
and take their weapons

. . . .

Airplane poems, rrrrrrrrrrrrrrr
rrrrrrrrrr . . . tuhtuhtuhtuhtuhtuh
. . . rrrrrrrr . . . Setting fire and
death to whities ass. Look at the
Liberal Spokesman for the jews clutch
his throat and puke himself into eter-
nity . . . rrrrrrrr. There's a negroleader pinned to a bar stool in Sardi's
eyeballs melting in hot flame Another
negroleader on the steps of the white
house one kneeling between the sheriff's
thighs negotiating cooly for his people.
Agggh . . . Stumbles across the room . . .
Put it on him, poem. Strip him naked to
the world! Another bad poem cracking
steel knuckles in a jewlady's mouth.[1]

At the same time it is possible, with a certain squint of the
eye, to see an integral relationship between the black experience as chronicled in recent literature and the aspects of anguish, absurdity, and sensuality dealt with in our previous
essays. The anguish is there aplenty, though it tends more
often than not to fall short of tragic proportions. The black's
old role of music-hall comedian, as fall guy and butt of the
joke, comes back on him at inopportune moments, vitiating

1. LeRoi Jones, *Black Magic: Collected Poetry, 1961–1967* (New York: Bobbs-
Merrill Co., 1969), pp. 116–17.

the sense of classical tragedy. As in Lonne Elder's *Ceremonies in Dark Old Men,* we don't get far enough from the barbershop and the soft-shoe shuffle to achieve a heroic dimension. Absurdity is even easier to remark. It is there in the basic incongruity of black life in a white society. The shantytown cradled among multi-million-dollar interstate highway projects, the jivecat Charlies in cheap zootsuits riding the subways of Manhattan, the white-haired old porters carrying bags and turning on air conditioners for prosperous white hotel guests, the patient-faced, stolidly built maids dotting Southern suburban streets in late afternoon, waiting for buses to take them back to their own world for the night—the absurdity is there. Ralph Ellison caught it particularly in *The Invisible Man* and set it to jazz, so that the absurdity had to stand out like a black funeral marching through ten million white neighborhoods all at once. Arrabal never wrote anything zanier, even though Ellison only took hard, cold reality and gave it a syncopated beat. And the sensuality is there in black writings too, permeating all of it. A rhythm, a mood, an odor, running through everything. There is no black equivalent of Monsieur Teste. Mind does not predominate in black writings, flesh does. Flesh and feeling and movement. A certain primitive wholeness still obtains, a unity of soul and body, which becomes thinnest when a writer becomes most aware of it; feeling his pulse, he makes it beat erratically; "infusing" sensuality, he makes it unreal.

Because of the highly cloistered or isolable nature of the black experience, the discernment of a metaphysical presence or otherness in it is of a different order from our undertaking in the three earlier essays. There the task involved defining a way of seeing what was not already visible or articulate, of recapturing the possibility of God, as it were, for a culture which has passed beyond the explicitness of a unified religious viewpoint into an almost helplessly pluralistic era. In black literature we are still dealing with a relatively stable constellation of religious attitudes and idioms, albeit at a

moment when that constellation is beginning to explode and
disintegrate in the manner of white Christianity in the
eighteenth and nineteenth centuries. What we find in black
writings, in other words, is a developing tension between a
relatively uncritical acceptance of traditional "Christian"
theology and a new, highly critical attitude which is as yet
largely untouched by either rationalism or philosophical
theology. The lines are drawn instead between what it means
to be a black man and what it means to worship a white God.
Where black is more and more dramatically defined as being
nonwhite, the idea of a deity conceived after the design of
"decadent white theology" is more and more untenable. The
very mood of liberation which grips the black imagination
today demands a God whose traits are African, and not
merely pale Semitic drawn through the siphon of sixteen centuries of Caucasian culture. As a character in N. R. Davidson,
Jr.'s play *El Hajj Malik* says, the white man raped African
women, forced his name on the new race, and taught it to
worship "an alien God having the same blond hair, pale skin
and blue eyes as a slavemaster."[2] And the obvious corrective
is voiced by a Muslim instructor in Marvin X's *The Black
Bird:* "Allah is God, The Only God—Allah is the Black Man
—Allah is your daddy! . . . The white man is the devil. . . .
Heaven is on earth."[3]

What *is* common between the perception of *présence* in
the earlier chapters and here is the way in which experience
itself becomes the ground for that perception. It is at the
limits of one's own being—what Karl Jaspers called the
"boundary situations"—that he encounters the transcendent.
The limits may be experienced in different ways—as tragic
circumstances, as the decline of a former order in one's affairs
or ways of viewing the world, as a sense of awe or wonder or
dread before the indissoluble and unabsorbable materialities

2. N. R. Davidson, Jr., *El Hajj Malik*, in Ed Bullins, ed., *New Plays from the
Black Theatre* (New York: Bantam Books, 1969), pp. 237–38.
3. Marvin X, *The Black Bird*, in Bullins, *New Plays*, pp. 112–15.

of his context, or even as a revolution in his social status, forcing a kaleidoscopic shift in his values, priorities, and responsibilities. Each is a way of encountering the self from a perspective transcending the self, and each becomes therefore an encounter with the Mystery and the Terror which, because of their aboriginal character, we have deigned to call God.

The turning point in black literature, when the former constellation began to disintegrate, appears to have come in 1940 with the publication of Richard Wright's *Native Son*. All the supraliterature, the literature *about* literature, is agreed upon that. There had been black protest literature before, by blacks as well as whites. W. E. B. DuBois, Frantz Fanon, Paul Dunbar, James Weldon Johnson, Langston Hughes, Claude McKay, Countee Cullen, Jean Toomer. The whole Harlem Renaissance. Wright had even published a book of stories, *Uncle Tom's Children*, in 1936. But there was something definitive about *Native Son*, something that caught the imagination of blacks and converted it to new uses. If a list of the most epoch-making books of the twentieth century is ever compiled, say by some desperate journalist trying to turn an article in the last copy of the last week of the last year of an era, that book, *Native Son*, will surely stand at or near the top.

Bigger Thomas. School dropout, juvenile delinquent, denizen of Chicago's Southside. Descendant of slaves. Last straw of the White Man's Burden. Self-consciously black and poor and resentful. Determined to "make it" in spite of the obstacles. His name no accident, said Leslie Fiedler, for he was more than Uncle Tom.[4]

The story, as Robert Bone has noted, was Dreiserian, like *An American Tragedy*.[5] Bigger was the product of the Amer-

---

4. Leslie Fiedler, *Waiting for the End* (London: Penguin Books, 1964), p. 118.
5. Robert Bone, *The Negro Novel in America* (New Haven: Yale University Press, 1958), pp. 142–43.

ican system, the spoilage of its dream. Sores fester, and sup-
purate; and he was the excrescence of our infection. Reared
in poverty worse than Clyde Griffiths', he wanted to move
in only one direction: out. Like Griffiths, he is introduced to
the other world—to affluence, society, power; only he is black
and can never really cross the line into that world the way
Griffiths did. Like Griffiths, his new situation is marred by a
series of accidents: he helps his employer's drunken daughter
to her room late one night, and, trying to keep her quiet with
a pillow to prevent discovery by her blind mother who has
entered the room, he unintentionally smothers her to death;
then, after what seems the most improbable event in the
novel, his burning the corpse in the furnace, he is found out
by a group of reporters who "happen" to be in the vicinity
of the furnace when it requires stoking and find some bone
fragments, which are identified as human remains by a reporter who "happens" to have studied medicine; and finally,
during his escape, he murders his girl friend Bessie and
throws her body down the air shaft of an abandoned tene-
ment building, discovering only afterwards that he forgot to
take his escape money from her pocket before doing so. Again
like Griffiths, he is visited in his cell by a faithful mother and
a minister, both intent upon his repentance and conversion
to a sustaining religious faith.

But unlike Griffiths, who became more or less reconciled
to his past, Bigger adamantly resists capitulation. The hate is
too immense, the injustice against his kind too long-smolder-
ing. He identifies the little crucifix the Negro preacher has
given him with the burning crosses of the Ku Klux Klan, and
feels it burning the skin of his chest. Hurling it away from
him, he shouts at the preacher, "Take your Jesus and go!"

Later, Bigger confides to his attorney, a Jewish communist
named Max, that he felt *free* for a little while after he killed
the women. (What did Eldridge Cleaver say in *Soul on Ice*,
that rape for him was "an insurrectionary act"?)

Max asks Bigger if he ever went to church:

"Yeah [says Bigger]; when I was little. But that was a long time ago."

"Your folks were religious?"

"Yeah; they went to church all the time."

"Why did you stop going?"

"I didn't like it. There was nothing in it. Aw, all they ever did was sing and shout and pray all the time. And it didn't get 'em nothing. All the colored folks do that, but it don't get 'em nothing. The white folks got everything."

"Did you ever feel happy in church?"

"Naw. I didn't want to. Nobody but poor folks get happy in church."

"But you are poor, Bigger."

Again Bigger's eyes lit with a bitter and feverish pride.

"I ain't that poor," he said.

"But Bigger, you said that if you were where people did not hate you and you did not hate them, you could be happy. Nobody hated you in church. Couldn't you feel at home there?"

"I wanted to be happy in this world, not out of it. I didn't want that kind of happiness. The white folks like for us to be religious, then they can do what they want to do with us."

"A little while ago you spoke of God 'getting you' for killing those women. Does that mean you believe in Him?"

"I don't know."

"Aren't you afraid of what'll happen to you after you die?"

"Naw. But I don't want to die."

"Didn't you know that the penalty for killing that white woman would be death?"

"Yeah; I knew it. But I felt like she was killing me, so I didn't care."

"If you could be happy in religion now, would you want to be?"

"Naw. I'll be dead soon enough. If I was religious, I'd be dead now."

"But the church promises eternal life?"

"That's for whipped folks."

"You don't feel like you've had a chance, do you?"

"Naw; but I ain't asking nobody to be sorry for me. Naw; I ain't asking that at all. I'm black. They don't give black people a chance, so I took a chance and lost. But I don't care none now. They got me and it's all over."[6]

6. Richard Wright, *Native Son* (New York: Harper and Row, 1966), pp. 329–30.

In the end Max proves to be a surrogate priest, helping the condemned Bigger to understand and accept his death. He explains the world in Marxian terms: property, vested interest, struggle, protection, revolt, repression. Bigger, he says, killed as a kind of protest against the closed system.

"The men who own those buildings are afraid. They want to keep what they own, even if it makes others suffer. In order to keep it, they push men down in the mud and tell them that they are beasts. But men, men like you, get angry and fight to re-enter those buildings, to live again. Bigger, you killed. That was wrong. That was not the way to do it. It's too late now for you to . . . work with . . . others who are t-trying to . . . believe and make the world live again. . . . But it's not too late to believe what you felt, to understand what you felt. . . ."[7]

Bigger responds to the picture Max has drawn. It explains the restlessness, the frustration, the anxiety he has always felt. He says he feels that what he did was "kind of right"—that he believes in himself now. "What I killed for must've been good!" he cries. "It must have been good!"[8]

There is a certain falseness in this conclusion. Nothing in Bigger has really prepared him for such a philosophical resignation, such a metaphysical ecstasy, as this. And there may be a kind of falseness in Max's assessment of things. Wright himself quarreled with the Communist party and left it in dissatisfaction about four years after this novel appeared.[9]

7. Ibid., p. 390.
8. Ibid., p. 392.
9. Wright was not the only major black writer to embrace Communism, of course; compare this segment of Langston Hughes's "Good-bye Christ," which appeared in the *Negro Worker* for Nov.-Dec., 1932:

> Christ Jesus Lord God Jehovah,
> Beat it on away from here now.
> Make way for a new guy with no religion at all.
> A real guy named
> Marx Communist Lenin Peasant Stalin,
> Worker ME—
> I said, ME
> Go ahead on now.
> You're getting in the way of things Lord
> And please take Saint Becton
> Of the Consecrated Dime

But there are many blacks and not a few whites, non-Communists as well as Communists, who have accepted this very depiction of the American dilemma, and who spiritualize their acts of rebellion in precisely the same fashion. *Native Son* has won a kind of biblical status in this regard. *The Autobiography of Malcolm X* and Cleaver's *Soul on Ice* both reflect the concept that property wrongs lie behind much of the American problem, and that the capitalist system has been built on the Negro as slave and chattel. And if anyone wants to read a recent book by a white man which is founded on essentially the same premise, he can see John R. Fry's *Fire and Blackstone*, which is surely the most astonishing collection of sermons and addresses ever published in this country. Fry is explicit: the role of the church today must be "to call into question every authority—law enforcement, courts, the political apparatus, the Mayor, realtors, the welfare Establishment, the Board of Education, local school officials—" and to keep doing it until the walls of Jericho fall down![10]

There is no question about it: *Native Son* is the fountainhead, the source of a radical new kind of black literature, afterward to be found in the writings of Ralph Ellison, James Baldwin, Chester Himes, Owen Dodson, Gwendolyn Brooks, John O. Killens, and LeRoi Jones. As Saunders Redding has said, "there is no present writer, that is, no Negro writer now at work, who has not felt the tremendous influence of Dick Wright."[11] Wright released the hate, resentment, and violence the Negro had been swallowing and smothering for centuries, and it could not be contained again. DuBois had

---

And step on the gas, Christ
Don't be so slow about moving;
Move.

(Cited by Benjamin E. Mays, *The Negro's God as Reflected in His Literature* [New York: Atheneum, 1969], p. 238.)

10. John R. Fry, *Fire and Blackstone* (Philadelphia: J. B. Lippincott Co., 1969), p. 92.

11. Saunders Redding, in *Anger, and Beyond*, ed. Herbert Hill (New York: Harper and Row, 1966), p. 204.

written in *The Souls of Black Folk* (1903) of the peculiar "double-consciousness" the Negro feels, the sense of always looking at himself through the eyes of white persons. "One ever feels his two-ness," he said: "an American, a Negro—two souls, two thoughts, two unreconciled strivings; two warring ideals in one dark body, whose dogged strength alone keeps it from being torn asunder."[12] For the first time in a celebrated novel (*Native Son* was the first book by a Negro to become a Book-of-the-Month selection) the desire for oneness, for a single-consciousness, became a prominent concern. Bigger Thomas was the prelude to black-is-beautiful, soul, and black power.[13] A long overdue therapy by overt expression was begun, and became a fact of public life in America. Laments, misgivings, recriminations, and virulent attacks against the white Establishment poured out, and the dammed-up tide of four hundred years shows few signs of abating in the near future.

The hatred and the violence. Is there a kind of theophany in them?

Ellison's *Invisible Man*, which Robert Bone thinks is "the best novel yet written by an American Negro" and "quite possibly the best American novel since World War II,"[14] pictures the humiliation young blacks suffer not only from whites, to whom they are always anonymous and invisible, but from the Establishment Negroes as well, the Uncle Toms and "screens" who hold their positions through docility and amenability to whites. Rejecting the naturalistic style of Flaubert, Zola, Dreiser, and Farrell, in which *Native Son* was written, for the impressionism of Joyce and Kafka and Faulkner, Ellison elevated the Negro struggle into a kind of mythi-

12. W. E. B. DuBois, *The Souls of Black Folk* (Chicago: A. C. McClurg & Co., 1903), p. 3.
13. Although Willie Ricks and Stokely Carmichael are often credited with having originated this phrase during a black march to Jackson, Mississippi, in the spring of 1965, Wright had in fact written a book of essays with the title *Black Power* in 1954.
14. Bone, *The Negro Novel*, p. 212.

cal quest not wholly unlike that of Joseph K. in *The Trial* or
K. in *The Castle*. Using the syncopations and improvisational
techniques of jazz as an actual prose device, he transmuted a
pathetic-humorous series of picaresque adventures into a picture of evil and the demonic whose general impact is utterly
stunning. There is an obvious relationship between his
scarred, disillusioned hero and the Underground Man of
Dostoevsky, Melville's Bartleby, Kafka's burrowing creatures,
and even the reticent figures of Beckett. Only in the case of
Ellison's protagonist there is a very specific antagonist: the
white man. The sense of injustice and cosmic debacle so real
and unbearable in the other writers becomes particularly in-
tolerable in *Invisible Man* because the agents of evil are so
incarnate and visible.

Baldwin, whose range of interests is wider and more sophisticated than Wright's was, so that the hatred sometimes
appears more diffuse or muffled in his works, nevertheless
writes tellingly of the antiwhite passions in some of his characters, as in this passage about Rufus Scott in *Another Country:*

He walked to the window and stood there, his back to Vi-
valdo. "How I hate them—all those white sons of bitches out
there. They're trying to kill me, you think I don't know? They
got the world on a string, man, the miserable white cock
suckers, and they tying that string around my neck, they killing
me." He turned into the room again; he did not look at Vi-
valdo. "Sometimes I lie here and I listen—just listen. They out
there, scuffling, making that change, they think it's going to
last forever. Sometimes I lie here and listen, listen for a bomb,
man, to fall on this city and make all that noise stop. I listen
to hear them moan, I want them to bleed and choke, I want
to hear them *crying*, man, for somebody to come help them.
They'll cry a long time before *I* come down there." He paused,
his eyes glittering with tears and with hate. "It's going to happen one of these days, it's got to happen. I sure would like to
see it." He walked back to the window. "Sometimes I listen to
those boats on the river—I listen to those whistles—and I think
wouldn't it be nice to get on a boat again and go some place
away from all these nowhere people, where a man could be

treated like a man." He wiped his eyes with the back of his hand and then suddenly brought his fist down on the window sill. "You got to fight with the landlord because the landlord's *white!* You got to fight with the elevator boy because the motherfucker's *white.* Any bum on the Bowery can shit all over you because maybe he can't hear, can't see, can't walk, can't fuck—but he's *white!*"[15]

A similar spirit flares out in *Tell Me How Long the Train's Been Gone* when Caleb Proudhammer and his parents are talking about what Caleb can do now that he is back from the war. His mother says he can do anything if he only makes up his mind that he is "just as good as they is"—*they* being the whites, of course.

> Caleb laughed. He mimicked her. "Just as good! Just as good as *who*—them people who beat my ass and called me nigger and made me eat *shit* and wallow in the dirt like a dog? Just as good as *them*? Is that what you want for me? I'd like to see every single one of them in their graves—in their graves, Mama, that's *right.* And I wouldn't be a white man for all the coals in hell."[16]

In an extraordinarily powerful short story called "Going to Meet the Man," Baldwin depicts the mistreatment of blacks through the eyes of a white lawman whose whole life has been a thing of fear since he was a boy and went to a "picnic" where a Negro man was lynched and castrated. Now the act of beating a black prisoner causes an involuntary erection of his penis, and sex and violence well up together in his unconscious like two monsters with a single body.[17] White people were astounded at the crimes of the Nazis against the Jews, said Baldwin in *The Fire Next Time,* but he doubted

15. James Baldwin, *Another Country* (New York: Dell Publishing Co., 1963), pp. 61–62.
16. James Baldwin, *Tell Me How Long the Train's Been Gone* (New York: Dell Publishing Co., 1969), p. 160.
17. James Baldwin, *Going to Meet the Man* (New York: Dell Publishing Co., 1966), pp. 198–218.

if the blacks were. "For my part," he said, "the fate of the
Jews, and the world's indifference to it, frightened me very
much. I could not but feel, in those sorrowful years, that this
human indifference, concerning which I knew so much already, would be my portion on the day that the United States
decided to murder its Negroes systematically instead of little
by little and catch-as-catch-can."[18] Leo Proudhammer, in *Tell
Me How Long the Train's Been Gone*, thinks, when he has
just heard the news that Hiroshima and Nagasaki have been
destroyed by A-bombs, "They didn't drop it on the Germans.
The Germans are white. They dropped it on the Japanese.
They dropped it on the yellow-bellied Japs."[19] There is a
flavor of demonic apocalypticism about this kind of thinking
—echoes of Armageddon and the suggestion of genocide—
which can proceed only from centuries of repression, enslavement, and anguish. It is no wonder that Baldwin feels that
there is not any love even in the black church,[20] and that the
black preachers, identifying with the Jews in bondage or in
exile, barely manage to veil their bitter hostility toward the
white pharaohs and taskmasters.[21]

Black author William Melvin Kelley takes a satirical approach to "the white problem" and shows how effective that
can be. In *dem*, a novel dedicated to "The Black people in
(not of) America," he draws a stinging caricature of white
life in the middle classes, and glorifies blacks by implying
that they possess the virtues which the whites lack. One particularly acerbic passage describes white lovemaking: it is
nervous, obligatory, ameliorated by peripheral concerns, and
lacking in orgasm. The woman says afterward, "Nothing was
happening to you. I could tell."[22]

18. James Baldwin, *The Fire Next Time* (New York: Dell Publishing Co.,
1964), pp. 74–75.
19. Baldwin, *Tell Me How Long the Train's Been Gone*, p. 280.
20. Baldwin, *The Fire Next Time*, pp. 56–59.
21. James Baldwin, *Notes of a Native Son* (New York: Bantam Books, 1968),
pp. 54–57.
22. William Melvin Kelley, *dem* (New York: Macmillan, 1969), pp. 13–14.

Kelley's opinion of the white man was caught adroitly by the artists, L. and D. Dillon, who drew the cover design for the Collier Books edition of *dem*. In the background, a bedroom, sits a white woman, dressed provocatively in a flouncy peignoir but with her hair up in a mushroom of curlers. In the corner of her boudoir mirror, barely visible, is the image of a neatly dressed, sombre, rather handsome Negro man—probably the object of the lady's sexual fantasies. In the foreground a Negro mammy is seated on a stool spoon-feeding a diminutive white man who is obviously dressed for his commuter ride to work, with his hat on, his attaché case in his hand, and his watch poised in prominent view on the tray of his high chair.

The former social inferiority of the Negro has been inverted, in the minds of some blacks, into a feeling of smugness and superiority, as though the whites somehow know less than they and could not get along without them. LeRoi Jones has articulated this viewpoint in a passage which I would call the Allegory of the Room: The white man keeps the Negro menial locked up in a room in his house and never enters that room. When the Negro comes out to clean the rest of the house, he remembers what he sees. Therefore only he has seen the whole of life in America—ghetto *and* suburb, hovel *and* mansion, maid's room *and* parlor.[23]

Because the Negro has seen "how it is" with the whites, he is now able to condemn his own attempt to become white and to ask why any colored man would even want to adopt such debilitating patterns of existence as those by which most whites live. Herbert Hill has noted the possible relatedness

23. LeRoi Jones, "Philistinism and the Negro Writer," in *Anger, and Beyond*, pp. 56–57. Jones adroitly uses this illustration to suggest that the white critic or reader has no right to say that his language and descriptions of things are obscene or pornographic, for the white man has not really seen life in the room. "So that a man who tries to tell me that I cannot have a character in a play say 'motherfucker' to describe something that my character sees is trying to deny the validity of a certain kind of experience and to deny the expression of that word as honest. He is quite clearly trying to deny a whole world of feeling because he does not know what the word means or how it is used" (p. 57).

of two separate articles which appeared in the same issue of the *New York Times* in the spring of 1965, one on the front page describing massive arrests in Selma of demonstrators opposing white supremacy, and the other on the inside back page reporting a marked and mysterious increase in the incidence of asthma among Negroes in this country; clinical psychologists have known for years of the relationship between emotional factors and the appearance of asthmatic attacks.[24] And Baldwin, denying the proposition that the four-hundred-year travail of the American Negro "should result merely in his attainment of the present level of the American civilization," said in *The Fire Next Time* that "I am far from convinced that being released from the African witch doctor was worthwhile if I am now—in order to support the moral contradictions and the spiritual aridity of my life—expected to become dependent on the American psychiatrist. It is a bargain I refuse."[25]

It is an entirely natural development, in light of everything else, that the more militant blacks should now have turned on white religion, particularly as manifested in black churches, and rejected it as a white man's device for keeping the Negro in submission and bondage through the years. The charge they make is essentially the one Marx made about the Christian religion in the entire Western world: it is an opiate which drugs the masses into acceptance of unbearable hardships in this world for the promise of better conditions in another world that is to come. As Wright said in *Native Son* of the sounds wafting up from a little church to the ears of Bigger Thomas in the room where he was hiding from the police, "the music sang of surrender, resignation."[26] And as Bigger said to Max, eternal life is "for whipped folks."[27]

24. Hill, *Anger, and Beyond*, pp. xx–xxi.
25. Baldwin, *The Fire Next Time*, pp. 129–30.
26. Wright, *Native Son*, p. 237. The scene anticipates the one in John Updike's *Rabbit, Run* in which Harry Angstrom stares out of a prostitute's room at a church gathering across the street.
27. Ibid., p. 330.

LeRoi Jones points out in *Blues People* that the Negro in America had to turn to the white man's religion for the simple reason that his own African religions were invariably ridiculed and usually forbidden. "Conjuring" and "hoodoo" and "devil talk" were punishable by whipping and even death. Certain practices and superstitions went underground or were assimilated into more acceptable forms of worship and belief, but in general the black man had simply to accommodate himself to a whole new religious pattern.[28] And Jones cites Fannie Kemble's journal of 1838 and 1839 in her observations that the white evangelicals of the nineteenth century who were so zealous for the black man's "soul" cared nothing whatever for his physical welfare, ignoring that completely.[29]

Christopher Hall, the big, black friend of Leo Proudhammer in *Tell Me How Long the Train's Been Gone*, says to Kenneth King, a young white man from Kentucky who has accused him of oversimplifying the race problem by blaming the whites for everything: "I'm not blaming you. You had a good thing going for you. You'd done already killed off most of the Indians and you'd robbed them of their land and now you had all these blacks working for you for nothing and you didn't want no black cat from Walla Walla being able to talk to no black cat from Boola Boola. If they could have talked to each other, they might have figured out a way of chopping off *your* heads, and getting rid of *you*." Smiling and taking a sip of his drink, Christopher continues: "So you gave us Jesus. And told us it was the *Lord's* will that we should be toting the barges and lifting the bales while you all sat on your big, fat, white behinds and got rich."[30]

The church, of course, provided something of importance to the blacks. As E. Franklin Frazier points out in *The Negro*

28. LeRoi Jones, *Blues People* (New York: William Morrow and Co., 1968), pp. 32–33.
29. Ibid., pp. 36–37.
30. Baldwin, *Tell Me How Long the Train's Been Gone*, p. 355.

Church, it afforded them whatever cohesion they actually retained as a race. And as Brink and Harris suggest in *The Negro Revolution in America,* it was one place where they could be persons and rise above the subhuman characterization placed on them by whites. In the church the black man "could at least find a brief surcease from slavery; there he could run his own affairs and worship as he pleased."[31] The scenes which Baldwin has described in *Go Tell It on the Mountain,* of wailing and moaning and dancing and singing in the Temple of the Fire Baptized, are similar to those in Negro literature for over a hundred years, and have been reenacted again and again in black churches throughout the country. The Spirit descends on the souls of black folk and they have their transports of joy and selfhood utterly sequestered from the eyes and criticism of white men.

But now there are black voices saying that this was all false, it was a charade, a delusion which the white man fostered just to keep the blacks submissive, to enable them to make their bricks without straw. The God they worshiped was really the white man's God, "the white God," as Rufus Scott called him in *Another Country.*[32] If God is not white, and if he really does love everybody alike, blacks as well as whites, asks Baldwin in *The Fire Next Time,* then "why are we, the blacks, cast down so far?"[33] In the dialogues with anthropologist Margaret Mead, *A Rap on Race,* Baldwin reminisces about his early life in the church and says he never understood white Christians. "I still don't," he says.

> I remember the photographs of white women in New Orleans, several years ago, during the school integration crisis, who were standing with their babies in their arms, and in the name of Jesus Christ they were spitting on other women's children, women who happened to be black, women with *their* babies in their arms. I have never been able to understand that

31. William Brink and Louis Harris, *The Negro Revolution in America* (New York: Simon & Schuster, 1969), p. 97.
32. Baldwin, *Another Country,* p. 24.
33. Baldwin, *The Fire Next Time,* p. 46.

at all. To put it in rather exaggerated primitive terms, I don't understand at all what the white man's religion means to him. I know what the white man's religion has done to *me*. And so, I could—can—accuse the white Christian world of being nothing but a tissue of lies, nothing but an excuse for power, as being as removed as anything can possibly be from any sense of worship and, still more, from any sense of love. I cannot understand that religion.[34]

"The Lord is my shepherd, and I *do* want," writes black poet Yusef Iman:

> The Lord is my shepherd and I do want.
>   So show me Lord, show me.
> Show me how to get the culture I had.
>   Show me Lord, show me.
> What is the language I use to speak, Lord.
>   Show me Lord, show me.
> How to get my people free.
>   Show me Lord, show me.
> How to get rid of fear, Lord.
>   Show me Lord, show me.
> How to get my people together, Lord.
>   Show me Lord, show me.
> To make them stop killing themselves.
>   Show me Lord, show me.
> To make them start loving themselves.
>   Show me Lord, show me.
> To make them unify themselves, Lord.
>   Show me Lord, show me.
>   Show me Lord, show me.
>   Show me Lord, show me.
>   Show me Lord, show me.
>   Lord I'm waiting.[35]

"That God you pray to," says Lil't, a character in Jimmy Garrett's play *We Own the Night*, to his mother, "is a lie. A punk. The last dick the whiteman's got to put in you."[36]

34. Margaret Mead and James Baldwin, *A Rap on Race* (Philadelphia: J. B. Lippincott Co., 1971), p. 86.

35. Yusef Iman, "Show Me Lord Show Me," in *Black Fire: An Anthology of Afro-American Writing*, ed. LeRoi Jones and Larry Neal (New York: William Morrow and Co., 1969), p. 386.

36. Jimmy Garrett, *We Own the Night*, in Jones and Neal, *Black Fire*, p. 536.

Poet Bobb Hamilton speaks directly to Whitey in "Brother Harlem Bedford Watts Tells Mr. Charlie Where It's At":

> Jeez man!
> How dumb do you
> Sombitches think we are?
> What happened to your God's justice?
> Speaking of justice
> Your god is a fink
> He let his own son get
> Lynched over there in
> Jerusalem Land
>   . . . .
> You a jive cat
> Charlie boy.
> You paid off some
> Rib picking Baptist Nigger preacher to
> Go around telling us
> To love you
>   everytime
> You kick our ass.[37]

The black preacher is a special object of contempt in several plays and novels because he is the immediate perpetrator of "smoked-up" white religion and is regarded by most whites as the logical arbitrator and keeper of the peace in interracial tension. Leo Proudhammer, in Baldwin's novel, rebukes his brother Caleb for "selling out" after the war and becoming a minister:

"Once, I wanted to be like you," I said. "I would have given anything in the world to be like you." I was crying. I hoped he couldn't see it, because of the rain. "Now I'd rather die than be like you. I wouldn't be like you and tell all these lies to all these ignorant people, all these unhappy people, for anything in the world, Caleb, anything in the world! That God you talk about, that miserable white cock-sucker—look at His handiwork, look!" And I looked around the avenue, but he didn't. He looked at me. "I curse your God, Caleb, I curse Him, from the bottom of my heart I *curse* Him."[38]

37. Bobb Hamilton, "Brother Harlem Bedford Watts tells Mr. Charlie Where It's At," in Jones and Neal, *Black Fire*, pp. 449–50.
38. Baldwin, *Tell Me How Long the Train's Been Gone*, p. 326.

In a far more humorous mood, though not necessarily less serious, is Ben Caldwell's play *Prayer Meeting, or, The First Militant Minister*, in which a burglar who is ransacking a black minister's apartment hides when the minister unexpectedly returns home. The minister comes in singing "What a friend we have in Jeee-sus." He talks to himself about what a strenuous day he has had, trying to console his people about the death of "brother Jackson" at the hands of a white policeman. They wanted vengeance, but he finally persuaded them that vengeance belongs to God, not man. As he talks, he begins to direct his words to God, and is praying. The burglar disgustedly tells him to shut up and get off his knees. He starts to come out of hiding, and then realizes that the minister thinks the voice is God's; so he remains closeted and talks to the minister as if he really were the Almighty. It is a marvelous comic opportunity to picture God-as-Black telling off a clerical Uncle Tom:

> You ain't worried 'bout what's gon' happen to your people. You worried 'bout what's gon' happen to you if something happens to your people. You so sure that if they go up 'gainst the white man they gon' lose and whitey won't need *you* no more. Or if they go up 'gainst whitey and win, then they won't need you. Either way yo' game is messed up. So you want things to stay just as they are. You tell them to do nothin' but wait. Wait and turn the other cheek. No matter what whitey do, always turn the other cheek. As long as you keep them off the white folks you alright with the white folks. MY PEOPLE got to keep catchin' hell so you can live like this! YOU STOP PREACHING AND TEACHING MY PEOPLE THAT SHIT! You better stop or I'll reveal myself and put somethin' on your cheeks![39]

Finally the minister says, "Lord, you keep saying 'my people.' Are black people your 'chosen people'?" "You goddam right!" says the burglar, "and you and everybody else better ack like it!"[40] While the minister is occupied with his praying, the

39. Ben Caldwell, *Prayer Meeting, or, The First Militant Minister*, in Jones and Neal, *Black Fire*, p. 591.
40. Ibid., p. 592.

burglar picks up his loot and slips out. The minister rises, puts down his Bible, takes out a revolver, and lays it beside the Bible. The next day he is seen standing before his people telling them that the time has come to put an end to all their suffering and exploitation at the hands of the white man.

This is slightly reminiscent of a far more earnest portrait of another black clergyman, Meridian Henry, in Baldwin's *Blues for Mr. Charlie,* a play loosely based on the Emmett Till murder case in Mississippi. It is suspected that Meridian's wife was killed by a white man in the hotel where she worked as a cleaning woman, and his son Richard has grown up hating the white race and despising his father for not taking any action at the time of his mother's death. Now Richard has come home from New York and been murdered by a white man for speaking freely to the white man's wife. After the trial of the white man, in which the state's attorney suggests that Meridian was indirectly responsible for his son's death because of his own less than fully "Christian" attitudes, the Negro minister takes the revolver his son had given him for safe keeping and places it under the pulpit with his Bible.

In the light of reminders like these, one can simply not give credence to Professor David Littlejohn's contention, in *Black on White,* a recent study of Negro writings, that there is "no 'Negro experience' in America"[41] or that the black author writes out of "the tight closet of the black imagination."[42] Even to whites, the accusations ring too true. It is no wonder that many blacks are in revolt against all the traditional values, including the white deity, and writing things like Charles Anderson's "Prayer to the White Man's God":

> I've been prayin' for centuries
> To some God up in the sky.
> Lord, what's the delay?
> Help me live today.

41. David Littlejohn, *Black on White: A Critical Survey of Writing by American Negroes* (New York: Viking Books, 1969), p. 157.
42. Ibid., p. 3.

God said, *Go 'way, boy*
I don't want to hear you cry,
But I know Jesus heard me
Cause he spit right in my eye.[43]

Some blacks have simply repudiated the idea of God and joined the ranks of materialistic or rationalistic atheists previously occupied primarily by whites. Richard Wright, for example, who confessed in his autobiography *Black Boy* that even as a child in the Negro church meetings he never quite came fully under the spell of religious belief, made his existentialist spokesman Cross Damon, in *The Outsider*, observe that "most men today are atheists, even though they don't know it or won't admit it. They live, dream, and plan on the assumption that there is no God. The full implications of this are enormous. It means that God no longer really concerns us as a reality beyond life, but simply as something projected compulsively from men's minds in answer to their chronic need to be rid of fear, something to meet the obscure needs of daily lives lived amidst strange and threatening facts."[44]

But this can hardly be representative of black thought as a whole. I do not think the basic religiosity of the Negro is a myth. His sensuality, for one thing, the directedness with which perception passes into feeling and feeling into perception, which Baldwin reports in *Nobody Knows My Name* to be much swifter in African Negroes even than in American Negroes, argues for a kind of essential spirituality about him which will not yield readily to intellectual agnosticism. The satirical conversation between two "darkies" in Wright's posthumously published *Lawd Today*, in which they talk matter of factly about "Gawd" and his omnipotence over creation,[45] is probably much more authentically black than the pseudo-

43. Charles Anderson, "Prayer to the White Man's God," in Jones and Neal, *Black Fire*, p. 191.
44. Richard Wright, *The Outsider* (New York: Harper and Row, Perennial Library, 1965), p. 359.
45. Richard Wright, *Lawd Today* (New York: Avon Books, 1963), pp. 165–70.

intellectual colloquys in *The Outsider*. As LeRoi Jones says in "Philistinism and the Negro Writer," there is something inviolably mystical at the heart of the Negro's being: "Mysticism is, after all, the hard core of Negro culture. . . . Yes, mysticism, because the spirit was always valuable—more valuable than *things* for the Negro because he never had anything. The religious core of Negro culture still remains, is present, even in Thelonious Monk or Ornette Coleman. They are trying to get at something which is finally spiritual and has to do with the transmitting of spirit rather than 'writing a biography,' which might be useful for some things, like trying to get a job."[46]

One alternative to the white man's religion is a radicalized kind of black religion. Marcus Garvey, the Negro leader of forty years ago who founded the Black Universal Negro Improvement Association and the African Orthodox Church, and who actually inspired a million followers in one of the first mass movements of Negroes in this country, talked about a black God, a black Christ, a black Madonna, and black angels. He had the kind of vision which would eventuate, in our own day, in a black theology and a black gospel.

Malcolm X told in his *Autobiography* how "a tall, blond, blue-eyed (a perfect 'devil') Harvard Seminary student" came to Charlestown Prison, in Boston, and lectured and conducted a question-and-answer period. The student had been talking about St. Paul. Malcolm raised his hand to ask a question. "What color was Paul?" he asked. And, without waiting for a reply, he kept on talking. "He had to be black . . . because he was a Hebrew . . . and the original Hebrews were black . . . weren't they?" According to Malcolm, the student flushed and finally replied "Yes." Malcolm wasn't through. "What color was Jesus . . . he was Hebrew, too . . . wasn't he?"

46. Jones, "Philistinism and the Negro Writer," in Hill, *Anger, and Beyond*, p. 58.

Both the Negro and the white convicts had sat bolt upright. I don't care how tough the convict, be he brainwashed black Christian, or a "devil" white Christian, neither of them is ready to hear anybody saying Jesus wasn't white. The instructor walked around. He shouldn't have felt bad. In all the years since, I have never met any intelligent white man who would try to insist that Jesus was white. How could they? He said, "Jesus was brown."

I let him get away with that compromise.[47]

It was only a short step from this notion, idly reborn in Charlestown Prison, to the full-fledged black gospel preached by Albert B. Cleage, Jr., a United Church of Christ minister and pastor of the Shrine of the Black Madonna in Detroit. Cleage's inflammatory vision, taking full advantage of what Cleaver has called "the furious psychic stance of the Negro today,"[48] can be sampled in *The Black Messiah*. "We must put down this white Jesus which the white man gave us in slavery and which has been tearing us to pieces," he says.[49] Jesus is not white but black. The hymn "Fairest Lord Jesus" ought to be rewritten "Darkest Lord Jesus."[50] Christianity as our fathers have known it is not the religion of Jesus at all, but the work of Paul and medieval white men.[51] The teaching that we should love all men, even our enemies, is a Pauline corruption of the real intention of Jesus, who was a black Zealot intent on overthrowing the white Roman government.[52] It isn't necessary to reject the Christian religion

47. *The Autobiography of Malcolm X* (New York: Grove Press, 1966), pp. 189–90.
48. Eldridge Cleaver, *Soul on Ice* (New York: Dell Publishing Co., 1968), p. 91.
49. Albert B. Cleage, Jr., *The Black Messiah* (New York: Sheed and Ward, 1968), p. 3.
50. Ibid., p. 35. Cf. comedian Dick Gregory's remarks in an article entitled "Divine Libel," in Robert S. Lecky and H. Elliott Wright, eds., *Black Manifesto* (New York: Sheed and Ward, 1969), p. 107: "Exhibit 'A' in a divine libel action would no doubt be a selection of the most popular pictures of Jesus adorning the walls of church sanctuaries and Sunday School classrooms throughout the nation. What price would God demand from the churches for having the audacity to lighten the color of his son's skin, straighten out his nappy hair, and portray him as a clean white hippie in a suburban setting?"
51. Ibid., p. 37.
52. Ibid., p. 96.

because it has been taught in a distorted fashion by white men; it is only necessary to get rid of the distortions, to find the true religion again, which is black.[53] Rap Brown is doing the kind of work Jesus did.[54] Black people ought not to complain about the looters who are taking from white folks, they ought to love them.[55] The looting is a mystical act, a celebrative act, the proof of this being that many looters take things they don't even want or need. They are simply caught up in the joy of God's great revolution.[56] As for God, he is surely disgusted with the blacks for crawling before white people for so long.[57] It is hard for him to lead people who are always waiting for him to intervene and take their part; this is not his way of working.[58] Now things are different. The black man is throwing off his self-hate.[59] Today the church "must reinterpret its message in terms of the needs of a Black Revolution. We no longer feel helpless as black people. We do not feel that we must sit and wait for God to intervene and settle our problems for us. We waited for four hundred years and he didn't do much of anything, so for the next four hundred years we're going to be fighting to change conditions for ourselves. This is merely a new theological position. We have come to understand how God works in the world."[60]

Marshall McLuhan, in *Understanding Media*, spoke of the strange alchemy involved whenever two unrelated entities or movements are brought into conjunction at a particularly propitious moment, like the printing press and the recovery of classical humanities; suddenly a third entity—in this case, the Reformation—emerges and transcends both of the prior entities. Is it possible that this phenomenon is occurring now

53. Ibid., pp. 104–5.
54. Ibid., p. 28.
55. Ibid., p. 18.
56. Ibid., p. 211.
57. Ibid., p. 112.
58. Ibid., p. 171.
59. Ibid., p. 7.
60. Ibid., p. 6.

with the combination of black religion and black power, that there has sprung from the coalescence a nationalistic movement whose force will be greater than the sum of the forces of the original elements? It does not appear at all unlikely that the blended black theology and black power, as Professor James H. Cone has called his book on the subject, tapping *both* the profound religious nature of the Negro and the impounded desire among blacks for freedom and social leverage, will become *the* fact to reckon with on the American scene in the decades just ahead.

Cone, who is generally less abrasive and explosive than Cleage, identifies black power as "Christ's central message to twentieth-century America."[61] The white church, because it has fostered teachings which at least supported oppression, even when they did not openly approve it, appears to be the enemy of Christ.[62] The "most corrupting influence" which white men had on the black church all along was "the 'white lie' that Christianity is primarily concerned with an otherworldly reality."[63] The real problem in America today, then, is not the black problem but the white problem,[64] and there is consequently "a desperate need for a *black theology*, a theology whose sole purpose is to apply the freeing power of the gospel to black people under white oppression."[65] "In more sophisticated terms this may be called a theology of revolution."[66]

There is not anything very new about this way of adapting the Christian religion to a particular cultural or sociological situation. It is perhaps the basic evangelical pattern throughout the centuries. Its precedents are to be found in the Christianizing of the West under the early missionaries; the move-

61. James H. Cone, *Black Theology and Black Power* (New York: Seabury Press, 1969), p. 1.
62. Ibid., p. 73.
63. Ibid., p. 121.
64. Ibid., p. 22.
65. Ibid., p. 31.
66. Ibid., p. 32.

ment of Islam, which was in the beginning a major Christian "heresy"; the clash and color and rivalries of the medieval crusades; the peasant revolutions of the later Middle Ages; the various reform movements in the era of the Renaissance; and the major evangelical thrusts of the last three hundred years. The magic always reappears whenever people discover a vivid personal identification with the biblical and redemptionist motifs and translate those motifs directly into their own contemporary situation as though there had been no intervening period of history and no cultural removal. Cone says the mistake of the "Death-of-God" theologians, William Hamilton and Thomas J. J. Altizer, was that they were looking in the wrong place when they discovered the irrelevance of religion: they should have been looking at the black man![67]

It is doubtful, of course, whether all blacks in this country will ever be caught up in a specifically black religion, or, for that matter, whether even a majority of them will. The idea of such a religion is probably a necessary radicalization for some, especially those herded together in the depressed areas of American cities. There is truth to Calvin C. Hernton's remark that "Violence, only violence, smoldering within the dark pits of the psyche, will at once be the tool of liberation as well as the experience which will create a sense of manhood and human worth within the souls of black folk."[68] And this truth applies, in its way, to religion. But there are many blacks who do not view the problem so simplistically, who tend to agree with James Baldwin when he says that the blacks and whites "deeply need each other" if they are to achieve their real identities, their true maturity, as human beings.[69] "We cannot be free until they are free," he says.[70]

There is a more complex viewpoint, and possibly, by virtue of that, a truer one. What is the relationship of black

67. Ibid., p. 71.
68. Calvin C. Hernton, "Dynamite Growing Out of Their Skulls," in Jones and Neal, *Black Fire*, p. 101.
69. Baldwin, *The Fire Next Time*, p. 131.
70. Ibid., p. 22.

fulfillment to white fulfillment, and vice versa? They are quite likely conjoined—inextricably so—in this country.

There is wisdom as well as terror in Leslie Fiedler's insight that much of the literature of this nation, white as well as black, deals in one way or another with the racial problem, and deals with it precisely because it is an obsession in the American unconscious. The white man carries an enormous sense of guilt in relation to the Indian first and then to the Negro. Somehow, says Fiedler, the colored man is tied to the white man's understanding, or preunderstanding, of the myth of the fall.

> It is clear, at any rate, that deep in the mind of America, if not actually below, at least at the lowest level of consciousness, there exist side by side a dream and a nightmare of race relations and that the two together constitute a legend of the American frontier, of the West (when the second race is the Indian), or of the South (when the second race is the Negro). In either case, it is the legend of a lost Eden, or, in more secular terms, of a decline from a Golden Age to an Age of Iron— as America moves from the time of the trapper to the days of the settler, the era of the great plantations to the days of Reconstruction. What makes the Golden Age golden, is, in the case of the Indian, as we have observed, an imagined state of peace between white man and red man, transplanted European and aboriginal at home: love, innocence, a kind of religious, even other-worldly calm, preside over this peace. And what makes the Iron Age iron is a state of war between redskin natives and paleface invaders: a burden of hatred and guilt, a history of scalpings and counter-revenges, make this war ultimate hell.[71]

The white man is not only aware that he has been the oppressor, he is aware that the oppressed are aware of it. Secretly, Fiedler implies, the wish of every white man now is to become colored, Indian or Negro, and merge his identity with that of the oppressed. If young people in this country are, in their whole life-style, their speech, their gait, the clothes they

71. Fiedler, *Waiting for the End*, p. 125.

wear, the music they love, even the vices they emulate, coming daily closer to the life-style of Negroes, it may be after all "what we have really longed for from the first."[72]

"In the very greatest American writers," says Fiedler, "in Melville, for instance, and Mark Twain, even (despite his embattled political position as a latter-day Southerner) in William Faulkner, we discover the full realization that until the American solves what he calls the 'Negro' or 'Indian problem,' the white American cannot be a whole man."[73]

This is essentially what Baldwin means when he says, in *The Fire Next Time*, that when whites have finally learned to accept and love themselves and each other "the Negro problem will no longer exist, for it will no longer be needed."[74]

Baldwin himself exhibits an interesting and somewhat complex instance of the developing black consciousness together with a more humane and complex theological viewpoint. A boy preacher who decided he would write instead of preach, and who, as Robert Penn Warren says, smuggled out the gift of tongues when he left the church,[75] Baldwin has for the most part been unwilling to concede to more radical blacks that white men are inherently evil, "devils," as Malcolm X called them, and that the black man's future depends on an abrupt and final severance from white culture. In a famous essay entitled "Everybody's Protest Novel," he discussed the Negro situation with special reference to Mrs. Stowe's *Uncle Tom's Cabin*, "that cornerstone of American social protest fiction," and Richard Wright's *Native Son*. Bigger is Uncle Tom's descendant, he said, "flesh of his flesh, so exactly opposite a portrait that, when the books are placed together, it seems that the contemporary Negro novelist and the dead New England woman are locked together in a

---

72. Ibid., p. 150.
73. Ibid., p. 139.
74. Baldwin, *The Fire Next Time*, p. 35.
75. Robert Penn Warren, *Who Speaks for the Negro?* (New York: Vintage Books, 1966), p. 280.

deadly, timeless battle," one "uttering merciless exhortations, the other shouting curses."[76] It is so futile, lamented Baldwin; they can only go on making thrust and counterthrust, black and white can, longing for "each other's slow, exquisite death," while "they go down into the pit together." We are all betrayed by this, he said:

> For Bigger's tragedy is not that he is cold or black or hungry, not even that he is American, black; but that he has accepted a theology that denies him life, that he admits the possibility of his being sub-human and feels constrained, therefore, to battle for his humanity according to those brutal criteria bequeathed him at his birth. But our humanity is our burden, our life; we need not battle for it; we need only to do what is infinitely more difficult—that is, accept it. The failure of the protest novel lies in its rejection of life, the human being, the denial of his beauty, dread, power, in its insistence that it is his categorization alone which is real and which cannot be transcended.[77]

Irving Howe, in an equally famous essay, "Black Boys and Native Sons,"[78] castigated both Baldwin and Ellison for "copping-out" on the Negro question, and insisted that all black fiction ought, by the very definition, to be "hate" fiction.

Baldwin has not been without hate. I have already cited passages from his novels which indicate his understanding of this emotional reaction in its severest forms.[79] But he is ob-

---

76. Baldwin, *Notes of a Native Son*, p. 17.

77. Ibid.

78. Irving Howe, "Black Boys and Native Sons," *Dissent* 10 (Autumn 1963): 353–68.

79. Add to these the speech of Richard Henry in *Blues for Mr. Charlie* (New York: Dell Publishing Co., 1964, p. 36), when his grandmother has just said that hatred is a poison: "Not for me. I'm going to learn how to drink it—a little every day in the morning, and then a booster shot late at night. I'm going to remember everything. I'm going to keep it right here, at the very top of my mind. I'm going to remember Mama, and Daddy's face that day, and Aunt Edna and all her sad little deals and all those boys and girls in Harlem and all them pimps and whores and gangsters and all them cops. And I'm going to remember all the dope that's flowed through my veins. I'm going to remember everything—the jails I been in and the cops that beat me and how long a time I spent screaming and stinking in my own dirt, trying to break my habit. I'm going to remember all that, and I'll get well. I'll get well."

viously drawn to something else, something beyond the mere resolution of the black problem, something the militant blacks must face if the revolution ever succeeds, is ever over: what it means to be a man, a human being, a *person* in the world. Just as the black theologians fashion their theology according to the immediate demand for and problems of a revolution, Baldwin has fashioned his in light of this more ultimate concern.

Several critics have noted that he has completely confused the matter of spiritual redemption with the discovery of sexual fulfillment, which means more specifically, in his case, homosexual relationships. Edward Margolies, for example, discussing *Giovanni's Room*, says that "beyond the particular successes and failures of the novel are the ways in which Baldwin has transmogrified his Christian vision into the ostensibly revolutionary subject matter of his novel. Christian love has here been transfigured into masculine love, the one redeeming grace in Baldwin's neo-Calvinist vision of a corrupt and depraved world."[80] And Robert Bone writes:

> In an effort to make Hell endurable, Baldwin attempts to spiritualize his sexual rebellion. Subjectively, I have no doubt, he is convinced that he has found God. Not the white God of his black father, but a darker deity who dwells in the heart of carnal mystery. One communes with this dark power through what Baldwin calls "the holy and liberating orgasm." The stranger the sex partner, the better the orgasm, for it violates a stronger taboo. Partners of a different race, or the same sex, or preferably both, afford the maximum spiritual opportunities.[81]

Bone says that Baldwin only imagines that this "new faith" constitutes a complete break with the past, that in fact "he has merely inverted the Christian orthodoxy of his youth."[82]

It is true that there is a relationship between sex and reli-

80. Edward Margolies, *Native Sons* (Philadelphia: J. B. Lippincott Co., 1968), pp. 115–16.
81. Bone, *The Negro Novel*, p. 238.
82. Ibid.

gion for Baldwin. Probably it was there subconsciously from
the beginning. It is obvious from the semiautobiographical
novel *Go Tell It on the Mountain* that the boy Jimmy Baldwin equated sinfulness and sexuality,[83] and the very imagery
of conversion which the adult novelist employed was unmistakably sexual:

> Then he whispered, not knowing that he whispered: "Oh,
> Lord, have mercy on me. Have mercy on me."
> And a voice, for the first time in all his terrible journey,
> spoke to John, through the rage and weeping, and fire, and
> darkness, and flood:
> "Yes," said the voice, "go through. Go through."
> "Lift me up," whispered John, "lift me up. I can't go
> through."
> "Go through," said the voice, "go through."
> Then there was silence. The murmuring ceased. There was
> only this trembling beneath him. And he knew there was a
> light somewhere.
> "Go through."
> "Ask Him to take you through."[84]

But who among us *hasn't* subconsciously connected sex
and salvation? Certainly St. Paul did, and Augustine, and
innumerable mystics during the Middle Ages. There is a
fairly recent Off-off-Broadway play by Tom Eyen called *The
White Whore and the Bit Player*, about a prostitute and a
nun, in which the nun very obviously relates to the large
cross on the stage as to a phallic object, and finally reveals
herself to be every bit as much a whore at heart as the actual
prostitute.

LeRoi Jones suggests that Negroes before the Civil War
did not connect promiscuity with sin, because random or
extraconjugal intercourse is not considered forbidden in
many pagan religions, but began to associate the two after

83. James Baldwin, *Go Tell It on the Mountain* (New York: Dell Publishing
Co., 1965), esp. pp. 18–19.
84. Ibid., p. 202.

the Reconstruction.[85] But certainly there are timeless traditions and mythologies in human culture suggesting the relationship, and Baldwin is hardly violating precedent if he has
indeed "confused" them.

There is more to it than that, however. Baldwin has sought
personal identity through sexual relationship; that much is
clear. And he has also come to interpret religion, God, spirituality, in terms of identity and self-realization. The reflections of Leo Proudhammer, in *Tell Me How Long the
Train's Been Gone*, when he considers how he can no longer
accept the white God of the old black religion, are doubtless
akin to the author's own feelings: "I had had quite enough of
God—more than enough, more than enough, the horror filled
my nostrils, I gagged on the blood-drenched name; and yet
was forced to see that this horror, precisely, accomplished His
reality and undid my belief."[86] He could reject the old God;
but he could not put off the new one, the one who transcends
the old one, who assumes him and discards him in the passing
of an era. God is *there* in the very metaphysics of human
horror, suffering, and guilt. We don't dismiss him; we only
hope, as someone has said—was it Eliot?—to grow up to him
in the end.

"I suggest," says Baldwin in *Nobody Knows My Name*,

> that the role of the Negro in American life has something to
> do with our concept of what God is, and from my point of
> view, this concept is not big enough. It has got to be made
> much bigger than it is because God is, after all, not anybody's
> toy. To be with God is really to be involved with some enor-
> mous, overwhelming desire, and joy, and power which you
> cannot control, which controls you. I conceive of my own life
> as a journey toward something I do not understand, which in
> the going toward, makes me better. I conceive of God, in fact,
> as a means of liberation and not a means to control others.[87]

85. Jones, *Blues People*, p. 92.
86. Baldwin, *Tell Me How Long the Train's Been Gone*, pp. 75–76.
87. Baldwin, *Nobody Knows My Name*, p. 113.

This is why there *is* a kind of spiritual affirmation about the relationship in *Giovanni's Room*. (Does it really matter that it is a homosexual relationship and not a heterosexual one?) As David, the white narrator of the novel says, "people can't, unhappily, invent their mooring posts, their lovers and their friends, anymore than they can invent their parents. Life gives these and also takes them away and the great difficulty is to say Yes to life."[88]

There is, it seems to me, a very great truth, a profound truth, one which both blacks and whites are struggling to realize today, in Baldwin's conclusion, that "if the concept of God has any validity or any use, it can only be to make us larger, freer, and more loving."[89]

There is a usefulness, among some blacks at least, for a black religion with a black theology and a black God. At this particular moment in the process of history, these serve an undeniable purpose. Even Baldwin would grant that. But the last lesson to be learned, the one Baldwin has managed to go on to while others have halted momentarily in the heat of the revolution, is this greater one, that God is more than any of us thinks he is, that he is more than the sum of the parts we have seen, and that what he *means* for us, in the final analysis, is the discovery of our ability to accept ourselves and others around us in this world. LeRoi Jones may say

> I want
> to see God. If you know
> him. Biblically, have
> fucked him. And left him wanting,
> in a continuous history of defeat.[90]

But the "history of defeat" is also a "history of victory." To be "taken in" is to penetrate the enemy; to be "eaten" is to get inside the eater. This is what incarnation is all about.

88. James Baldwin, *Giovanni's Room* (New York: Dell Publishing Co., 1956), p. 10.
89. Baldwin, *The Fire Next Time*, p. 67.
90. Jones, *Black Magic*, p. 62.

Epilogue

It was Rilke, in *The Notebooks of Malte Laurids Brigge*, who said that whenever one's name is spoken too often and by everyone it is time to take another—any other—in order to be free and to do one's work again. Possibly the same is true for a deity. As the Yahweh of Judaism and the Almighty of Christendom, our God has had a long and notorious history; so long and notorious, in fact, that it must now prove a considerable restriction to him.

Or at least it is a restriction to us. Having glimpsed him in one form or relationship, we assume it is the one most suited to him and simply cease to look elsewhere. In time, our idolatries cripple and impair the true religious instinct among us, betraying us into bigotries and intolerances of the worst sort. They effectually blind us to the sacramental nature of all that is, to what the English novelist and theologian Charles Williams called "coinherence," that continuous interaction between flesh and spirit which stitches all reality together, and imbues it with that meaning-approaching-joy which is the greatest desire of an enlightened mind.

For this reason, beyond all others, we need the artists in our society. It is they who unsettle us from our infantile visions and premature theologies. Iconoclasm is their business; stealing fire from the gods is their stock in trade; they live by the burnt offerings and sweetmeats ravaged from the Holy of Holies itself. It is they who are the real martyrs, they, not the orthodox churchmen and theologians, who usher us repeatedly into the inner sanctum, and, brushing aside gossamer veils, show us the *deus incognito*.

159

It is misleading for us to speak of art in the service of religion except in terms of this kind of violation. The adorning of sanctuaries, the designing of baptisteries, and the painting of saints' images have their place, of course, even as representations of official dogma. But it is only when the poets and artists are free to blaspheme, to enter the very jaws of sanctity and there pull our hallucinations' teeth, that they really conduct us into the presence of the Most High, or lead us to that baptism of spirit which men have called the New Birth. Transcendence is an impalpable quality discovered more often in risk and variation than in security and familiarity.

This is not to say that God is more present in the neglected and broken places of the human vista than in the smoother, more familiar ones—only that our sight is keener there, and our hearts more open. Perhaps it is a weakness of ours, but surprise was ever the most important ingredient of epiphany. It is the *shock* of recognition that makes it recognition. That is the real secret of incarnation and the way it works. We believe, as Tertullian said, not because it is rational and amenable to demonstration, but because it is absurd and conforms to the irregularities of our experience. We pledge ourselves to follow, not because the way is known or the goal remarked, but because we are gathered by the moment, galvanized by a single compelling image, drawn into the game before we know what has happened. Like Donald Barthelme, we trust the fragments, not the whole, because life itself always seemed finite, broken, and discontinuous.

We do well, therefore, to consider the visions of Lawrence and Miller and Picasso and all the other makers and seers of our time, not in order to dogmatize them—heaven save them from such a fate!—but in order to encounter in greater range and with more sensitivity the "stuff" of reality, the irreducible and implacable facts, from which theologies are fashioned. Sooner or later, our "terrible hunger for objects," as Roethke called it, gives way to fresh and revitalizing impressions of the anonymous, pseudonymous, eponymous One who both is and isn't among them, who both inhabits and transcends them, and engages us constantly in the hide-and-seek that makes life so wonderful and fascinating.

My friend whose letter I quoted in the Introduction did well to put off the God who was put off by Arnold and Huxley before him; it was time to reject that God. Putting off old gods is in fact indispensable to acquiring new ones.

But the God who once took a name, and flesh and figure, takes other names, other flesh, other figures. If we have learned anything about him, we have learned this. It is the substance of the gospel and the true meaning of the incarnation. This is why we must watch for him patiently, the way a hunter waits for his quarry; for where there is no vision, no sense of immediacy, the people perish. And it is why we must watch humbly, without hope of our orthodoxies; for the proud spirit never sees.

Index of Names

Adamov, Arthur, 73
Adams, Robert Martin, 8
Aeschylus, 11, 14, 36, 74
Albee, Edward, 16
Altizer, T. J. J., 151
Anders, Günther, 58
Anderson, Charles, 145
Anderson, Sherwood, 79, 102, 108
Anouilh, Jean, 74
Anselm, 80
Apollinaire, Guillaume, 57
Aristotle, 15–16, 23
Arnold, Matthew, 8, 10
Arrabal, Fernando, 66, 72, 127
Artaud, Antonin, 49–53, 57, 61–63, 74–75
Auerbach, Erich, 102
Augustine, 80, 156

Baldwin, James, 133, 135–137, 139, 140n, 141, 143, 145, 146, 151, 153–158
Dall, Hugo, 58, 108
Barth, John, 66
Barth, Karl, 86
Barthes, Roland, 34
Baudelaire, Charles, 3, 25
Beckett, Samuel, 4, 6, 33–37, 41, 48, 55, 69, 70–72, 74, 95–99, 123, 125, 135
Bellow, Saul, 103, 108
Bernanos, Georges, 66
Berry, Wendell, 101
Bodkin, Maud, 121
Bone, Robert, 129, 155
Bonhoeffer, Dietrich, 1, 2

Bonifazi, Conrad, 81
Bonnefoy, Claude, 54n
Brautigan, Richard, 6, 87, 103, 115–116
Breton, André, 57, 76, 108
Brink, William, 141
Brod, Max, 32
Brooks, Gwendolyn, 133
Brown, Norman O., 2, 80, 86, 123
Brown, Rap, 149
Bultmann, Rudolf, 2
Burke, Kenneth, 103
Burns, Robert, 9
Burroughs, William, 87

Caldwell, Ben, 144–145
Campbell, Joseph, 33
Camus, Albert, 1, 25, 27, 29–31, 32, 54–56, 74, 77, 84–86, 96, 108
Carlyle, Thomas, 101
Carmichael, Stokely, 134n
Cassie, David, 10
Chardin, Teilhard de, 76
Chuang Tzu, 37
Cleage, Albert B., Jr., 148–149, 150
Cleaver, Eldridge, 130, 133
Coe, Richard, 34
Coleman, Ornette, 147
Coleridge, S. T., 27
Cone, James H., 150, 151
Cox, Harvey, 2
Crane, Stephen, 103
Cullen, Countee, 129

Dante, 116
Davidson, N. R., Jr., 128
Descartes, René, 54, 96
Desnos, Robert, 57, 108
Dillon, L. and D., 138
Dodds, E. R., 39
Dodson, Owen, 133
Dostoevsky, Fyodor, 3, 21–22,
    29, 32, 55, 64, 91, 135
Dreiser, Theodore, 25, 103, 134
DuBois, W. E. B., 129, 133
Duchamp, Marcel, 56
Dunbar, Paul, 129
Durrell, Lawrence, 87

Eckhardt, Meister, 116
Elder, Lonne, 127
Eliot, George, 87
Eliot, T. S., 1, 6, 7, 25, 38,
    87–88, 157
Elizabeth I, 18
Ellison, Ralph, 55, 127, 133,
    134, 154
Else, Gerald F., 15n
Emerson, Ralph W., 82, 84,
    101, 106
Esslin, Martin, 72–73, 74
Euripides, 74
Eyen, Tom, 156

Fanon, Frantz, 129
Farrell, James T., 134
Faulkner, William, 1, 134, 153
Fiedler, Leslie, 129, 152–153
Fitzgerald, Edward, 8
Flaubert, Gustave, 134
France, Anatole, 113
Frazier, E. Franklin, 140
Freud, Sigmund, 23, 33, 60, 108
Fromm, Erich, 47
Fry, John R., 133
Fuller, Edmund, 1

Gardner, Dame Helen, 13, 14,
    14n, 23, 38, 39
Garrett, Jimmy, 142
Garvey, Marcus, 147

Genet, Jean, 67–68, 72
Gheorghiu, Virgil, 3
Gide, André, 94
Ginsberg, Allen, 87
Grass, Günther, 6
Gray, Thomas, 8

Hall, Edward T., 2
Hamilton, Bobb, 143
Hamilton, William, 143, 151
Hamsun, Knut, 91
Hanna, Thomas, 84, 86
Hardy, Thomas, 1, 8, 25, 87
Harris, Louis, 141
Hegel, G. F. W., 54
Heidegger, Martin, 6–7
Heller, Joseph, 66, 74
Hemingway, Ernest, 1, 25, 66,
    102, 103
Henry VIII, 18
Hernton, Calvin, 151
Hesse, Hermann, 2, 40, 82–84
Hill, Herbert, 138
Himes, Chester, 133
Hoffer, Eric, 2
Hoffman, Frederick, 4–5, 103,
    116
Hopkins, Gerard Manley, 121,
    122
Housman, A. E., 8
Houston, Jean, 115
Howe, Irving, 154
Hughes, Langston, 129, 132 n
Huizinga, Johan, 109–110
Huxley, Aldous, 2, 11–12, 40,
    46
Huxley, T. H., 8

Iman, Yusef, 142
Ionesco, Eugène, 53–54, 55, 57,
    59, 65, 74, 99, 123
Ivanov, Vyacheslav, 21

James, Henry, 102
Jarrell, Randall, 103
Jarrett-Kerr, Martin, 3

Jaspers, Karl, 128
Jesus, 8, 10, 13, 45, 71, 76, 148
Jewett, Sara Orne, 101
Johnson, James Weldon, 129
Jones, LeRoi, 125–126, 133,
    138, 140, 147, 156, 158
Joyce, James, 6, 34, 110, 111,
    116, 134
Jung, C. G., 47

Kafka, Franz, 6, 31–33, 55,
    57–58, 59, 64, 66, 73, 74, 75,
    134, 135
Kahler, Erich, 38
Keats, John, 6, 8
Keen, Sam, 4, 80, 122
Kelley, William M., 137–138
Kemble, Fannie, 140
Kenner, Hugh, 35n, 95
Kerouac, Jack, 87, 115
Kesey, Ken, 66, 72, 115
Kierkegaard, Søren, 30, 55, 77,
    80
Killens, John O., 133
Knox, Bernard, 16
Krieger, Murray, 25, 46

Laotse, 7
Lautréamont, Comte de, 25
Lawrence, D. H., 81, 84, 86–88,
    92–93, 95, 99–101, 109, 114,
    116, 117–122, 160
Leary, Timothy, 2
Leavis, F. R., 87, 88, 100–101
Lewis, H. D., 106
Lewis, R. W. B., 107
Littlejohn, David, 145
Luther, Martin, 64, 80
Lynch, William, 34, 41

Malamud, Bernard, 25, 27–29
Malcolm X, 133, 147–148, 153
Mallarmé, Stéphane, 6
Mann, Thomas, 91
Marcuse, Herbert, 2
Margolies, Edward, 155
Marlowe, Christopher, 11

Marvin X, 128
Marx, Karl, 139
Maslow, Abraham, 2
Masters, R. E. L., 115
Mauriac, Claude, 66
McGill, Arthur, 89
McKay, Claude, 129
McLuhan, Marshall, 2, 40, 149
Mead, Margaret, 141
Melville, Herman, 3, 25, 26–27,
    55, 135, 153
Merleau-Ponty, M., 79
Merton, Thomas, 114
Mill, J. S., 8
Miller, Arthur, 38, 46
Miller, Henry, 87, 90–92, 102,
    111–114, 116, 125, 160
Miller, J. Hillis, 5
Monet, Claude, 104
Monk, Thelonius, 147
Montagu, Ashley, 81

Nabokov, Vladimir, 87
Nietzsche, Friedrich, 1, 91

Ong, Walter, 15
Otto, Rudolf, 26

Paul, 14, 148, 156
Phillips, J. B., 70
Picasso, Pablo, 160
Pinter, Harold, 58–59, 63
Pirandello, Luigi, 52
Pope, Alexander, 15, 64
Pound, Ezra, 110
Protagoras, 18, 64
Proust, Marcel, 52, 96, 97

Redding, Saunders, 133
Richards, I. A., 19
Ricks, Willie, 134n
Ricoeur, Paul, 47
Rilke, Rainer Maria, 159
Rivière, Jacques, 49–53, 55,
    57, 62
Robbe-Grillet, Alain, 23–25,
    30, 39, 41, 48, 80, 84, 116

Robinson, John A. T., 2
Roethke, Theodore, 103–4,
    122, 160

Sarraute, Nathalie, 41
Sartre, Jean-Paul, 1, 74, 80, 83
Schreiner, Olive, 1, 87
Scott, Nathan A., Jr., 6, 26,
    103–4, 117
Sewall, Richard B., 12, 13,
    14n, 16, 39
Shakespeare, William, 8, 11,
    13, 14, 18–21, 22, 32, 33, 36,
    37, 41, 42, 59
Shelley, Percy B., 8
Simpson, N. F., 68–69
Snodgrass, W. D., 103
Sophocles, 14, 16–18, 32, 36,
    41, 74
Steiger, Rod, 43, 44, 47
Stein, Walter, 18–21
Stevens, Wallace, 104–7
Stoppard, Tom, 37
Stowe, Harriet B., 153
Stuart, Jesse, 101

Tanner, Tony, 101–2, 107–8
Tennyson, Alfred Lord, 8

Tertullian, 160
Tezuka, 7
Thompson, Lawrance, 26
Thoreau, Henry David, 101,
    106
Tillich, Paul, 1, 2, 77, 80, 92,
    106
Toomer, Jean, 129
Twain, Mark, 3, 102, 153

Updike, John, 139n

Valéry, Paul, 51, 93–95, 97

Wallant, Edward, 43, 47
Warren, Robert Penn, 153
Weil, Simone, 10
Whitman, Walt, 102
Widmer, Kingsley, 114n
Williams, Charles, 159
Wolfe, Thomas, 103
Wolfe, Tom, 2
Wordsworth, William, 82, 85
Wright, Richard, 129–34, 135,
    139, 146, 153

Zola, Émile, 134